TIME

THE MAKING OF AMERICA

Life, Liberty and the Pursuit of a Nation

By the Editors of TIME

THE MAKING OF AMERICA
Life, Liberty and the Pursuit of a Nation

EDITOR	Kelly Knauer
DESIGNER	Ellen Fanning
PICTURE EDITOR	Patricia Cadley
WRITER/RESEARCH DIRECTOR	Matthew McCann Fenton
COPY EDITOR	Bruce Christopher Carr

ACKNOWLEDGMENT

Three stories in this volume are based on articles that previously appeared in different form in TIME magazine's *Making of America* series. They are: Ben Franklin profile, by Walter Isaacson; "Go Fry a Kite," by Frederic Golden; "Across the Wide Missouri," by Landon Y. Jones.

TIME INC. HOME ENTERTAINMENT

PUBLISHER	Richard Fraiman
EXECUTIVE DIRECTOR, MARKETING SERVICES	Carol Pittard
DIRECTOR, RETAIL & SPECIAL SALES	Tom Mifsud
MARKETING DIRECTOR, BRANDED BUSINESSES	Swati Rao
DIRECTOR, NEW PRODUCT DEVELOPMENT	Peter Harper
ASSISTANT FINANCIAL DIRECTOR	Steven Sandonato
PREPRESS MANAGER	Emily Rabin
BOOK PRODUCTION MANAGER	Jonathan Polsky
MARKETING MANAGER	Kristin Walker
ASSOCIATE PREPRESS MANAGER	Anne-Michelle Gallero

SPECIAL THANKS TO

Bozena Bannett, Alexandra Bliss, Glenn Buonocore, Bernadette Corbie, Brian Fellows, Suzanne Janso, Joe Lertola, Robert Marasco, Brooke McGuire, Ilene Shreider, Adriana Tierno

ISBN: 1-932994-08-4
Library of Congress Control Number: 2005904461

TIME Books is a trademark of Time Inc.

We welcome your comments and suggestions about TIME Books. Please write to us at
TIME Books • Attention: Book Editors • PO Box 11016 • Des Moines, IA 50336-1016

If you would like to order any of our hardcover Collector's Edition books, please call us at 1-800-327-6388
(Monday through Friday, 7 a.m.–8 p.m., or Saturday, 7 a.m.–6 p.m., Central time).
PRINTED IN THE UNITED STATES OF AMERICA

TIME

THE MAKING OF AMERICA

Life, Liberty and the Pursuit of a Nation

How 13 Fragile Colonies United to Defy an Empire
And Create the World's First Great Democracy

By the Editors of TIME

Contents

Benjamin Franklin • George Washington • Abigail Adams

James Madison

Thomas Jefferson

Alexander Hamilton

The Making of America

AFTER RECEIVING THE SURRENDER OF BRITISH troops under General Charles Cornwallis at Yorktown, Va., General George Washington wrote a letter announcing the great victory and addressed it to the President of the United States. We can well imagine the pleasure with which America's first President, Joseph Hanson, received it. It might be a bit harder for us to imagine that the first President of the U.S. was not Washington but rather Hanson, who took office on Nov. 5, 1781, served out his one-year term, then yielded to a succession of six other Presidents who struggled to hold the fledgling Union of squabbling ex-colonies together. But that is indeed the case.

As it happened, that first attempt to govern the United States of America, under the Articles of Confederation and Perpetual Union, survived for only seven years, considerably short of perpetuity. The Articles of Confederation provided the Federal Government with too little authority to maintain law, order and equality among the new states. So America's best minds came together once again in Philadelphia, where they had declared their independence from Britain 11 years before, and hammered together a far better government for themselves, creating a Constitution that has served Americans well for more than 200 years now. It was under this new rule of law that George Washington took office as President in 1789.

The saga of this false start illustrates the central theme of this book: America was made, not born. The United States was the first nation in history to be consciously designed from scratch by the hand of man. This nation is not the result of long centuries of social and political evolution: rather, it was wrestled out of the abstract realm of ideas by a process of argument and debate, shaped into articles and amendments on paper, then enacted through inaugurations, elections and legislation. And if the government was broken, as it clearly was in the 1780s, well, it was Americans' job to fix it.

Willed into being by the Founding Fathers, who heeded Ben Franklin's call to "Join, or die," the U.S. and its Constitution are not finished products or sacred immutable scripture; they are works in progress, always capable of amendment and improvement. And that's why the subject of the making of America is not history for today's Americans: rather, it is breaking news, current events, the stuff of headlines, blogs, talk radio shows and countless letters to the editor.

As this book was in preparation, Americans were preoccupied by the fate of a brain-damaged Florida woman, Terri Schiavo, and were hotly debating the rights of the individual vs. the responsibilities of the government. At the same time, Senate wrangling over President George W. Bush's federal judiciary nominees launched Americans into a furious set-to over the proper balance between the Judicial, Executive and Legislative branches of the government, echoing positions first staked out by James Madison and Alexander Hamilton in 1787. Meanwhile,

JOIN, or DIE.

First Amendment issues dominated the headlines, whether the subject was freedom of religion, in the form of the ongoing debate over prayer in the schools; freedom of the press, in the concerns over journalists' right to protect their sources; or freedom of speech, in the argument over whether or not to extend the Patriot Act. When it comes to the founding principles and structures of American life, William Faulkner's words get it just right: "The past is never dead. It isn't even past."

This sense that the Constitution is urgently, compellingly alive today—that it remains a primary shaper of our lives and fortunes—helps explain why Americans in recent years have made best sellers of biographies of Hamilton, Franklin, John Adams and other Founding Fathers, and even of a scholarly volume that explores the shifting relationships among these brilliant men, Joseph Ellis' *Founding Brothers*. Likewise, when TIME began devoting an annual Fourth of July issue to the subject of the making of America, readers responded with enthusiasm: letters poured in, and this demonstration of renewed interest in the founding years of the nation led to the publication of this book.

Our account of the making of America begins with the passage of the Stamp Act by Britain in 1765 and encompasses the first 50 years of America's independence, concluding with the deaths of Adams and Thomas Jefferson on the 50th Anniversary of the Declaration of Independence, on July 4, 1826. We hope you enjoy it.
—*Kelly Knauer, 2005*

Ben Franklin designed the political cartoon at left, urging colonial unity. At right, the mythical figure of Columbia crowns the head of George Washington, first President under the Constitution of 1787

mind, [advancing] to keep pace with the times." —Thomas Jefferson

Colonists march to oppose the Stamp Act in 1765

Defying an Empire

THE FOLLY OF ENGLAND
AND THE RUIN OF AMERICA

The Colonies: 1754-74

1754
French and Indian War in Ohio River Valley; George Washington leads Virginians fighting French

1760
Colonial population: 1.5 million; George III becomes King

1763
Pontiac leads Indian confederation in rebellion in far-Western territories

1764
Britain's Sugar Act raises levies on colonial commerce

1765
Britain passes Stamp Act and Quartering Act; colonists unite in Stamp Act Congress and boycott British goods

1766
The Stamp Act is repealed

1767
Townshend Acts impose new, onerous taxes on colonies

1768
Sam Adams' Circular Letter calls for colonial unity; Britain sends troops to enforce order in Boston

1769
The Virginia Resolves oppose taxation of colonies without representation

1770
Colonial population: 2.2 million: five colonists killed in Boston Massacre; Townshend Acts repealed

1773
Tea Act takes effect; colonials protest in the Boston Tea Party

1774
Coercive Acts (Intolerable Acts) punish Massachusetts; First Continental Congress meets in Philadelphia

Young George Washington

"I had four bullets through my coat, and two horses shot under me, yet

Go West, Young Man

FIRST, FORGET EVERYTHING YOU KNOW ABOUT George Washington. For most Americans, that won't be too hard: of all the Founding Fathers, Washington remains the most remote and unapproachable; we carry him in our pockets, enshrined in the almighty dollar bill, but we don't carry him in our hearts. He lacks Thomas Jefferson's breadth and mystery; Alexander Hamilton's dramatic death-by-duel; Ben Franklin's twinkle. Biographer David McCullough even managed to turn prickly, preachy John Adams into a sympathetic character, but Washington awaits the novelist or screenwriter who can make us care about him, even if it's self-evident which actor should play him in a future blockbuster: Russell Crowe.

So imagine George Washington as a young Virginian of 16, taking the classic American journey, west into the wilderness—at that time, just over the Blue Ridge Mountains of the Shenandoah Valley. Young George's father, a farmer and member of the minor Virginia gentry, had died when his son was only 13. But the lad benefited from good connections; he had been invited on this western surveying trip by his wealthy neighbors, the Fairfaxes.

Washington loved it all. Although not to the log cabin born, he became as much a man of the frontier as Andrew Jackson or Abraham Lincoln, taking up surveying as his occupation. Then, in 1753, with the French and Indian War raging, the Governor of Virginia asked the 21-year-old to lead a detachment of men to the Forks of the Ohio (now Pittsburgh) to take on the French, who were building a fort to control the critical confluence of the Ohio and Allegheny rivers. Washington, unschooled in strategy, made a hash of the assignment: he built a fort in a poor location that was quickly overwhelmed by the French, and he was even briefly taken prisoner.

Two years later, Washington returned to the Ohio Valley as a colonel, serving under British General Edward Braddock, who insisted on fighting the French and Indians in the close-ranked European style. The Britons and Americans were ambushed and devastated, but Washington led his men bravely and escaped the rout—with four bullet holes in his coat. His coolness under fire made him a celebrated figure in the British Empire. Already, this giant of a man (6 ft. 3 in.) was showing the gravitas and air of command that would make him a born leader of men; all who met him were struck by his noble bearing. These transforming days on the frontier would carry the Virginian to greatness. ∎

escaped unhurt, altho' death was levelling my companions on every side of me!"

Benjamin Franklin

"It is unreasonable to imagine that printers approve of everything they print."

The Sage of Reason

LIKE WALT WHITMAN, ANOTHER OUTSIZED AMERICAN ICON, Ben Franklin contained multitudes. America's premier scientist, humorist, business strategist, statesman and diplomat, he was the Founding Father made of flesh, not marble. He proved by flying a kite that lightning was electricity, and he invented a rod to tame it. He devised bifocal glasses and clean-burning stoves and theories about the contagious nature of the common cold. He was a pioneer of do-it-yourself civic improvement, launching such schemes as a lending library, volunteer fire corps, insurance association and matching-grant fund raiser. He helped invent America's unique style of homespun humor and philosophical pragmatism. And he was the person most responsible, of all the founders, for instilling in the new nation the virtue that is central to its role in the world struggle: religious tolerance.

Ben Franklin is the only Founding Father we feel comfortable referring to by a nickname, and he was more enthusiastic about democracy than were most of his compatriots. Some feared and hated "the Mob"; Franklin had faith in the wisdom of the common man. Through his self-improvement schemes for furthering the common good, he helped to create a new ruling class of ordinary citizens tolerant of their neighbors.

At age 12, Franklin became an apprentice at the printshop of his older brother James, a tough master. "I fancy his harsh and tyrannical treatment of me," Franklin later speculated, had the effect of "impressing me with that aversion to arbitrary power that has stuck to me through my whole life." The surest guard against such power, he came to believe, was free expression, the free flow of ideas and a free press—a point he proved in print with his newspaper, the *Pennsylvania Gazette*.

Sent to Paris as the colonies' envoy during the Revolution, Franklin proved himself a master of diplomatic realism, playing an adroit balance-of-power game among France, Spain, the Netherlands and Britain. Yet he was also a great image-maker, who cast himself to the French as a symbol of virtuous frontier freedom: a fur cap served as his badge of homespun simplicity. Healthy, wealthy and wise, he lived to 84, the unclassifiable, unmatched *ur*-American. ∎

JOHN SINGLETON COPLEY, CA. 1770–72—MUSEUM OF FINE ARTS, BOSTON—TIME LIFE PICTURE COLLECTION

Rebel Rouser

DON'T BE FOOLED BY THIS IMAGE, IN WHICH the gifted portraitist John Singleton Copley makes Samuel Adams appear to be the embodiment of formality and reserve, a Washington of the North. In fact, Sam Adams was a hothead and firebrand; like Ben Franklin's new invention, the lightning rod, he seemed to be a conduit for outsized energies. Born in Boston in 1722, Sam—a cousin of the far more prudent John Adams—graduated from Harvard, then failed in a series of occupations. Inheriting his father's debt-laden business as a supplier of malt to brewers, he ran it into complete bankruptcy. The man who would later lead the insurgency against British taxes then took a job as Boston's top tax collector and made a hash of that as well; in 1765 he resigned his office, handing the city a major shortfall of £8,000; the city treasurer sued and won a judgment against him, which Boston later forgave.

If unsuccessful in business, Adams anticipated and mastered the mantra of modern-day revolutionaries: organize. In the long process that led the colonists from anger against Britain to the tipping point of revolution, Adams, like his compatriot Paul Revere, was what contemporary author Malcolm Gladwell terms a "connector," a gifted networker who spread his revolutionary message in ever-wider circles. In Boston he was an active participant in the town meeting and Caucus Club, a founder of the Sons of Liberty and a chief "Indian" in the Boston Tea Party. In Massachusetts he served as a representative in the legislature, writing and helping pass the Circular Letter that denounced the 1767 Townshend Acts. As his fame spread across the colonies, he helped forge the growing links among the freedom-minded as a founder of the Committees of Correspondence, and in 1776 he became a proud signer of the Declaration of Independence. While a student at Harvard he had considered joining the clergy; years later he found his calling in preaching revolution. ∎

Samuel Adams

"If ye love wealth greater than liberty, the tranquillity of servitude greater than the animating contest for freedom, go home from us in peace"

Patrick Henry

"[When] a King ... degenerates into a Tyrant, [he] forfeits all right to his subjects' obedience"

Seasoned in Treason

TAUNTS OF "TREASON" HAUNTED PATRICK HENRY'S CAREER. The young Virginia lawyer first gained renown in 1763, when he won his county's case against a group of Anglican clergymen who had received their full salaries—reckoned against the profits of the local tobacco crop—despite a drought that drove up "sotweed" prices and thus the clerics' pay. When Henry, then 27, called King George III a "tyrant" for allowing such injustice, voices charging "Treason!" rang out. The judge paid no heed—he was Patrick's father, Colonel John Henry—and the jury ruled against the clergy and the Crown.

Lively, impulsive and impolitic, the eloquent Patrick Henry was later elected to Virginia's House of Burgesses just in time to shepherd the Virginia Resolves through a rump session of the legislature. Five radical resolutions denouncing the 1765 Stamp Act, the Resolves were hailed and soon copied all across the colonies. "Caesar had his Brutus, Charles I his Cromwell," Henry thundered in championing the resolutions, "and George III may profit by their example." Shouts of "Treason!" erupted from the gallery at this invocation of regicide, but Henry defiantly replied, "If that be treason, make the most of it."

Henry certainly made the most of his growing fame as a Tidewater Samuel Adams. Named a delegate to the First Continental Congress in 1774, he was one of the gathering's most radical voices. When war came, he joined Virginia's militia to face down Lord Dunmore, the British Governor, in a dispute over gunpowder, then served five terms as Governor himself after independence was declared. Ardent in defense of states' rights, he deplored the 1787 Constitution's federal focus and turned down President Washington's 1795 offer to serve as Secretary of State, preferring liberty to diplomatic death. ∎

America's Last King

DENOUNCED AND DEMONIZED BY COLONIAL patriots and often falsely portrayed today as an incompetent lunatic, King George III of Britain was a complex, tragic figure rather than a human cartoon. The third in the line of Hanoverian monarchs who first ascended the throne in 1714, George reigned for six decades, from 1760 to 1820. A lover of books and a devoted natural scientist, he took a special interest in agriculture; critics mocked him as "Farmer George." But if some of his interests seem downright Jeffersonian, the King never doubted that his divine duty was to rule Britannia's empire. Conscientious and deeply involved in matters of state, he attempted to win back some of the royal prerogatives lost over time to Parliament, without success. In times of crisis, whether opposing his ministers or his colonies, he displayed a mulish inflexibility that often aggravated the situation; he refused even to receive the Olive Branch Petition of 1775, the moderate colonists' last offer to settle the rebellion without bloodshed.

Perhaps the King's greatest failing was his inability to see the colonists as a remarkable new breed of alert, independent thinkers; instead, he consistently treated them as wayward children who must be cuffed back into line. His decision to employ German mercenaries against his own subjects pushed many colonists who had previously considered themselves loyal to the throne directly into the patriot camp.

Although Americans think of George III as a failure, during his long reign Britain consolidated its stance as the world's foremost power and defeated its great enemy, Napoleon Bonaparte. The King did suffer periodic bouts of mental instability, whose cause remains unresolved. By 1811 his disorders had become so pronounced that he was forced to yield rule to a regent, his son, the future George IV. In his last 10 years, King George was transformed into King Lear; blind and mad, His Majesty was an object of pity and terror. ■

King George III

"A traitor is everyone who does not agree with me."

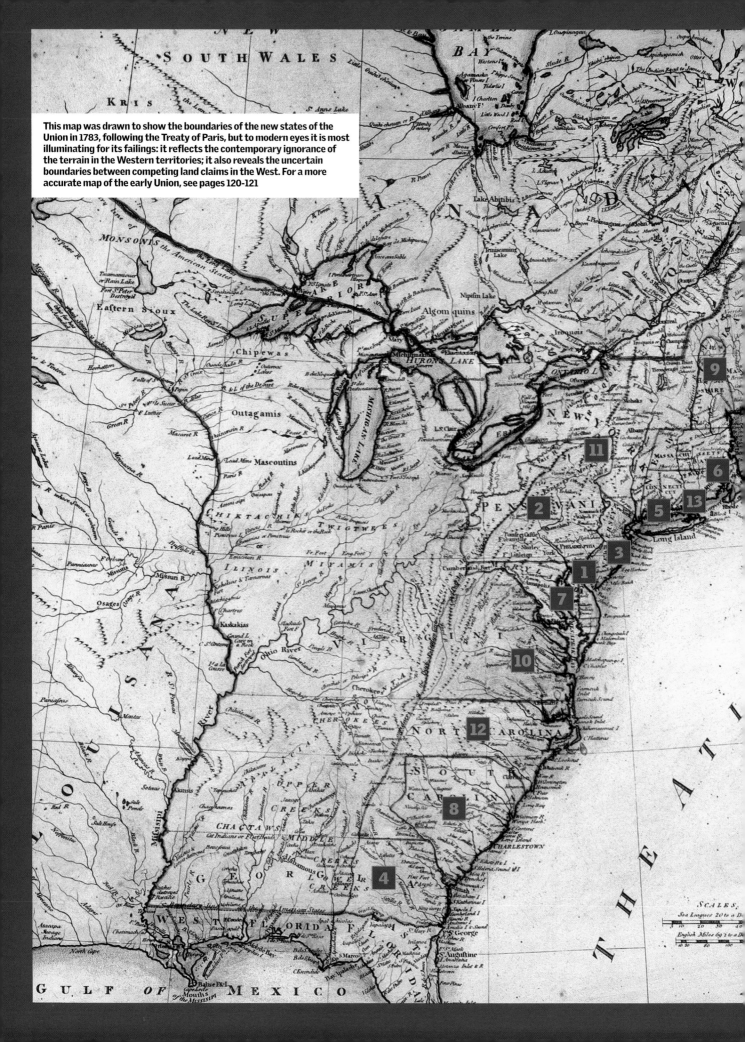

This map was drawn to show the boundaries of the new states of the Union in 1783, following the Treaty of Paris, but to modern eyes it is most illuminating for its failings: it reflects the contemporary ignorance of the terrain in the Western territories; it also reveals the uncertain boundaries between competing land claims in the West. For a more accurate map of the early Union, see pages 120-121

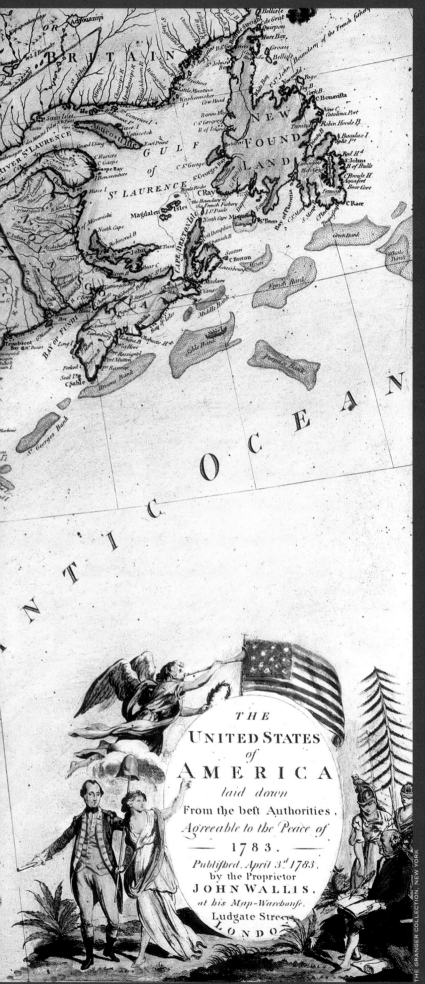

Worlds Apart

The 13 British colonies that united in 1776 to declare their independence from the Crown were distinct in heritage, geography, commerce and religion. Distance hampered communication; trade battles fostered rivalries; competing land claims bred bad blood. In short, as late as 1755, there was little to suggest that this mixed bag of settlements would ever find unity. A summary of the colonies' heritage (in order of their later admission to the Union) outlines the chasms that had to be bridged to transform the divided colonies of America into the United States of America.

1. Delaware Settled: 1638. Founded by Dutchman Peter Minuit (for Sweden), it was seized by the Netherlands, which yielded it to the British, who made it part of Pennsylvania (to Maryland's anger). Named after an early colonial Governor of Virginia, Lord de la Warr.

2. Pennsylvania Settled: 1643. The Crown awarded William Penn this colony (once home to Dutch and Swedes) to encourage Quakers to leave Britain. "Penn's Woods" fostered religious toleration and brotherly love.

3. New Jersey Settled: 1633. Named for the Isle of Jersey (of which one of its founders, Sir George Carteret, was Governor); the colony's real estate, trade potential and natural resources drew settlers.

4. Georgia Settled: 1732. The colony was carved from the Carolinas by King George II (its namesake) to create a buffer between Spain's holdings to the south. Many first settlers were debtors working toward freedom.

5. Connecticut Settled: 1635. Named for the Algonquin word Quinnehtukqut ("Beside the Long Tidal River"), it was founded by Thomas Hooker, who was driven out of Massachusetts for his tolerant religious views.

6. Massachusetts Settled: 1620. It was colonized by Pilgrims and, later, Puritans fleeing oppression by the Church of England; their intolerance led to the founding of New Hampshire, Rhode Island and Connecticut.

7. Maryland Settled: 1634. Charles I granted Lord Baltimore its charter as a haven for British Catholics; it is named for the King's wife, Queen Mary. An outpost of religious tolerance, it also pioneered tobacco as a crop.

8. South Carolina Settled: 1670. A Spanish colony here in 1526 lasted only a single year; 144 years later, English settlers moved in from Barbados. After Charles II separated Carolina from Virginia, the colony split apart in 1729 owing to agricultural rivalries.

9. New Hampshire Settled: 1623. Given as a Crown grant to John Mason (from Hampshire, England), it was settled by refugees from Massachusetts Puritans.

10. Virginia Settled: 1607. The first colony began as a business venture; only 60 of its original 900 settlers survived. Named for Elizabeth, the "Virgin Queen"; its House of Burgesses was the first representative assembly in the British colonies.

11. New York Settled: 1624. The jewel in the crown of Dutch holdings in the New World; when the British seized the colony in 1664, James, the Duke of York (brother of King Charles II) renamed it after himself.

12. North Carolina Settled: 1653. King Charles II gave loyal nobles this large slice of territory from Virginia; in Carolina (from "Carolus," Latin for Charles), farmers grew rice in the north, tobacco in the south.

13. Rhode Island Settled: 1636. Roger Williams, banished from Massachusetts for advocating the separation of church and state, founded this most tolerant of the original 13 colonies.

Left to right, George Washington oversees his fields in Virginia; a Philadelphia street scene, 1775; a frontier family in the West

A New World, Divisible

The **13 British colonies** in America are frequently at odds, until Britain's misguided rule sends a compelling message: Come together, right now

THE FIRST CHAPTER OF THE STORY OF THE MAKING OF America covers the 10 years between 1765-75, roughly the period between the Stamp Act and the first British-American skirmishes at Lexington and Concord. The events of this period center around a single grand theme: the growth of a sense of unity among the heterogeneous British settlements in America, a mental evolution summed up in the Latin phrase engraved on the penny, *e pluribus unum:* out of many, one. The development of this shared sense of a common destiny among formerly disparate colonies and individuals was the beginning of the process that led directly to the Declaration of Independence in 1776 by a new entity on the world stage, a confederation of former colonies calling itself the United States of America. If we are to appreciate the efforts of those who bridged the divide between *pluribus* and *unum,* we need to begin by measuring the divide.

In 1763 the British succeeded in driving the French out of North America in the great war of empires that Europeans call the Seven Years War and Americans call the French and Indian War. At this time the British colonies along the Atlantic Coast of North America were a clutch of dissimilar settlements. Each colony was its own small world, and the differences among their residents far outpaced their similarities: colonists worshipped in different churches, grew different crops, lived in very different environments, worked at different trades. Only 150 years removed from the first British settlements in the New World, most Americans were still strangers in a strange land, more interested in building a future for themselves and their children than in creating a new nation.

In the 1760s the colonies made up a fascinating, diverse pageant of humanity: beaux and belles flirting in Savannah and Philadelphia; Yankee sea captains sailing out of New Bedford in search of whales; lawyers in powdered wigs and knee breeches arguing cases in Richmond and Boston; black slaves from equatorial Africa acclimating to new lives in Maryland and Georgia; Puritan preachers condemning slavery in Massachusetts; butchers, bakers and candlestick makers hiring apprentices in Charleston and Baltimore; merchants and traders competing for business in New York City—and everywhere along the vast reaches of the frontier, wives in homespun, raising children and crops while their husbands hunted, fished, bartered for goods and cleared the land.

Along the edges of the wilderness lived the original Americans, the Indians who had been pushed back into the forests by the tide of European settlement. Although these Native Americans had forged alliances with both the British and French during the recent war, they represented an unstable element, subject to no organized colonial or Crown power,

"Then join hand in hand, brave Americans all! By uniting we stand, by

that further made life in the colonies unpredictable, dangerous and troubled.

Divided by geography, religion, economy, heritage and, in some cases, language—many German speakers, for instancee, were settling in Pennsylvania—these first Americans did not regard themselves as united and had no reason to. In fact, many of them did not yet primarily identify themselves as "American": they thought of themselves as British citizens living in North America and defined themselves by their colony, as Virginians, Rhode Islanders or New Yorkers.

The colonies were also far from equal in size and riches. Some of them were enormous: all of Carolina was divided out of the first British colony, vast Virginia, by royal fiat; then this new colony split apart again to form North and South Carolina. Some of them were tiny: Rhode Island was an afterthought in the grand scheme of colonial settlement, and its size reflects that fact. Some colonies, like Virginia, New York and Connecticut, were "landed": they claimed vast territories stretching west beyond the Allegheny Mountains to the Mississippi River; other colonies were "landless": their charters from the Crown left them with no room to grow.

Some colonies, like Pennsylvania, Maryland and Massachusetts, had been founded on a sense of religious mission: William Penn called Pennsylvania a "holy experiment." Others, like New Jersey and New York, had been established with an eye to commerce and trade. One deep colonial division would chart the future of the nation: some colonies, especially the great agrarian colonies of the South, were already deeply reliant on the slave trade by the 1760s; other colonies, mostly in the North, had little need for slaves.

That the residents of this crazy quilt of mismatched settlements would ever come to view themselves as one people seems utterly unlikely. Yet the colonies did come together, and it was that great uniter of men—a common enemy—that did the trick. Britain was that enemy. Its mismanagement of the colonies took many forms over many years, yet all its mistakes reflect a single monumental misperception: the King and his ministers failed to understand that in carving a society out of a wilderness, the Americans had shaped themselves into a new breed of men. This new man was an independent spirit who already possessed the germ of what we now call the American Dream: he was an optimist who believed he could shape with his own hands a future better than the past, unlimited by Britain's age-old barriers of class and custom.

The colonists enjoyed a great advantage remarkable for its absence rather than its presence: they were liberated from the burdens of the past. The New World was originally a geographical term, but it can be seen to stand for something larger. In this new land, a new kind of life was being created, in which individual men were free agents, capable of forging their own futures, unhobbled by the confines of the old, rigid structures of Europe. This New World had seen no Middle Ages; it was home to no dukes, earls or princes of the church. It was a tabula rasa, where ambitious, hardworking men could write their own ticket; and when it came time for them to write their own government, there were few vested interests outside the Crown to oppose them.

This frontier world bred exhilarating new habits of mind, encouraging self-reliance and rewarding initiative. Is it any wonder that when, two years after the end of the French and Indian War, Britain's Parliament began ordering Americans to jump, the colonists refused to ask, How high? ∎

dividing we fall." —John Dickinson, patriot, *The Liberty Song of 1768*

Old State House

"Otis was a flame of fire ... Then and there was the first scene of the first act of opposition to the arbitrary claims of Great Britain." —John Adams

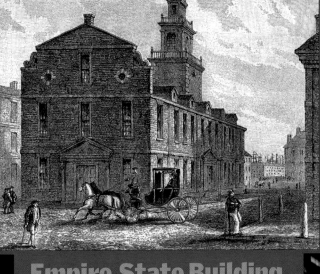

Empire State Building

In 21st century Boston, the Old State House is a small fish in a big pond. Surrounded, outnumbered and dwarfed by modern skyscrapers, it is a perfect analogy for the relationship between Bostonians and the British in the turbulent years of the 1760s and '70s, when the American colonists gradually came to feel dominated by their mother country and began taking up arms against the world's greatest empire. But if the building reminds us today of the rebels' David-and-Goliath plight, it once played just the opposite role: in the years before the Revolution, this was the seat of British rule in Massachusetts and a hated symbol of imperial oppression.

In those years, Boston became the forge of rebellion, and this building, erected in 1713, was at the center of events. Here, in 1761, American lawyer James Otis argued in court against the Writs of Assistance, which allowed British soldiers—redcoats—to search Americans without a warrant; John Adams, then a student, called Otis "a flame of fire." Real fire came nine years later: the Boston Massacre took place just beneath the balcony at left. Six years later, on July 18, 1776, the Declaration of Independence was first read from that same balcony, after which patriots tore the last hated insignia of British rule from the building.

By 1881 the Old State House was derelict and forlorn; incredibly enough, it was almost bought by Chicagoans, who proposed to dismantle it brick by brick and move it to Illinois. Citizens formed the Bostonian Society, which raised the funds to preserve it—saving precious memories of the Revolution, while possibly averting a second War Between the States. ∎

Led by the Sons of Liberty, Bostonians ransack, then burn, the elegant home of British Lt. Governor Thomas Hutchinson on Aug. 26, 1765

Burning Down the House

Strapped for funds to defend the colonies' expanded borders, Britain imposes a new tax, but the **Stamp Act** ignites protests—and domiciles

B Y THE 1760S, BRITAIN AND HER AMERICAN COLONIES were like an aging husband and wife who had drifted apart. No longer fully able to remember what had brought them together in the first place, each one sure that anything said will be misunderstood, they strove mightily to ignore each other. But each partner in this marriage grown stale still needed something from the other.

Britain's cupboard was bare, depleted by the French and Indian War, in which England wrested from France control of Canada and vast new lands west of the present colonies, extending to the Mississippi. Frequent skirmishes with Native Americans along these new frontiers, home to the prosperous fur trade newly inherited from the French, led London to de-

cide that more than 10,000 British troops would be permanently garrisoned in America, along with several British warships. And surely the colonists, who would most immediately benefit from the troops' presence, ought to help defray the expense of transporting, housing and feeding them?

The colonials begged to differ. Stung by a growing if not yet fully articulated sense that they did not enjoy the same rights as other British subjects (for example, to elect members of Parliament), they saw no need for a standing British army in their midst. Many suspected the troops were being sent to intimidate them; these redcoats were little more than foreign occupiers. Moreover, colonists suspected Britain's real aim was to reduce the debt it incurred fighting a European war; Amer-

"No law can be made or abrogated without the consent of the people by

icans viewed the French and Indian War as merely the North American theater of the larger global conflict history calls the Seven Years' War.

The English thought the Americans ungrateful: at a time when the average annual tax paid by a British subject was 26 shillings, the typical resident of Massachusetts contributed only one shilling to the royal treasury. Unfortunately for the British, the means they settled on to support the new troops—a levy on printed documents called the Stamp Tax—betrayed a startling lack of insight into the mindset of their overseas brethren. Indeed, London could not have devised a strategy more guaranteed to outrage the colonists and unite them in opposition.

Passed unanimously by Parliament on March 22, 1765, and scheduled to go into effect in November of the same year, the Stamp Tax required that an official wax seal be affixed to documents ranging from newspapers and legal briefs to deeds and bills of sale—54 categories of everyday printed material in all. Depending on the kind of document, colonial bureaucrats would charge anywhere from a few pence to several pounds for this seal. The bitter opposition of lawyers and newspaper editors, property owners and merchants—in short, nearly every citizen of some influence in the colonies —was guaranteed.

The Stamp Act came on the heels of a series of hated tax measures. The previous year, the Sugar Act had increased levies on sugar, coffee, wine, textiles and dyes shipped to the colonies from England, while the Currency Act had banned colonial governments from issuing their own paper money, making American merchants dependent on British banks.

The new act crossed an entirely new threshold: it was the first measure that required colonists to pay money directly from their own pockets into the British treasury. To make matters worse, Parliament also enacted the Quartering Act in the same month as the Stamp Act, requiring colonists to house and feed the British troops they despised.

AMERICANS ERUPTED IN DISSENT. BY THE SUMMER OF 1765, local chapters of a secret organization, the Sons of Liberty, had been formed in most of the colonies. The group organized boycotts of British goods and staged protest rallies, some of which escalated into violence. In August, Boston's stamp tax collector, Andrew Oliver, was hanged and burned in effigy. Confronted by this sight, a terrified Oliver tried to retreat to his home—only to find it a smoldering ruin. In the same month, the home of Massachusetts Gov-

An illustration in a Philadelphia newspaper (above) portrayed the wax seal called for by the Stamp Act (below) as a death's-head. Opposition to the revenue act united very different colonies against a common foe. In Virginia, Patrick Henry railed against the levy in the House of Burgesses. In Massachusetts, a brilliant young lawyer named James Otis—who would later coin the phrase "Taxation without representation is tyranny"—ominously declared before the colony's Superior Court that previous arbitrary exercises of power had "cost one King of England his head and another his throne." Watching Otis from the gallery that day was a young law student named John Adams, who would later write, "Then and there the child Independence was born."

ernor Thomas Hutchinson was burned to the ground. A few days later in New York, arsonists burned the home of a British officer who had vowed that he would "would cram the stamps down American throats at the point of his sword." When the Governor of New York threatened to order his troops to fire into a rioting crowd, he received a written message predicting that he would be hanged from the nearest lamppost within a few minutes of doing so. Throughout the colonies, stamp-tax collectors resigned their posts and, in more than a few cases, ran for their lives.

The Stamp and Quartering acts led to calls for an assembly in which representatives of each colony would meet, independent of British oversight, to discuss common goals. When the Stamp Act Congress convened in New York on Oct. 7, 1765, nine of the 13 colonies were represented; Virginia, North Carolina and Georgia abstained, while New Hampshire declared it would sign any agreement the others ratified. Ten days later, the Congress issued a resolution declaring in part that it "is inseparably essential to the freedom of a people, and the undoubted right of Englishmen, that no taxes be imposed on them, but with their own consent, given personally, or by their representatives."

On Nov. 1, when the Stamp Act officially went into effect, many colonies observed a symbolic (and slightly histrionic) day of mourning: businesses closed their doors, while long-faced men solemnly paraded through the streets, dressed in funeral garb. The English were already looking for a way out. Of the 13 colonies, only Georgia even attempted to enforce the measure. All the other colonies either quietly ignored it or, in the case of rambunctious Rhode Island, openly declared the law invalid. In London, British merchants smarting from the colonial boycott were also calling for the law's repeal.

In February 1766, the perplexed British government invited that most reasonable of Americans, Benjamin Franklin, to articulate the colonists' position. Members of Parliament were stunned to hear the first citizen of the colonies, who was not given to exaggeration, warn of a possible revolution if the British used their army to enforce the Stamp Act. By the following month, His Majesty's government had had enough: on March 17, Parliament repealed the Stamp Act. It was a victory for the colonies in the increasingly fractious relationship between two peoples that, by then, had little love remaining for each other but were still locked in the cold embrace of custom and language, law and property. ∎

Bullets and Broadsides

Embattled British troops pull the trigger under pressure, killing five Americans, and rebels turn the **Boston Massacre** into a cause célèbre

"[The British troops] formed and marched with insolent parade, drums

LIKE A SMALL CHILD WHO HAS FACED DOWN THE SCHOOL-yard bully, the American colonies were pumped up with newfound self-regard in the late 1760s. They had forced the most powerful nation in the world to back down over the Stamp Act and had learned a dangerous lesson: violence succeeded. Riots in Boston, New York City and elsewhere had put British troops on the run and forced the repeal of a slew of onerous tax laws, with not one American life lost.

Where this would likely lead was not lost on the British. In 1767 British Chancellor of the Exchequer Charles Townshend proposed the series of new tax laws that would bear his name, intending to humble the colonies as much as to raise revenue. The new levies on paper, paint, lead, glass and tea enraged the colonists they were meant to cow. Emboldened by their recent success against the Stamp Act, the colonists renewed

their boycotts against British goods and once again began harassing the Crown's customs inspectors and tax collectors. This time, instead of backing down, London sent troops.

On Oct. 1, 1768, more than 4,000 British soldiers landed in Boston, a city with a population of just 16,000. From the day the occupation force arrived, the scent of incipient bloodshed was in the air. Bostonians provoked the soldiers with constant taunts, threats and low-grade assaults. The hated British infantry, professional soldiers, followed strict orders to avoid violence but indulged in displays of arrogance and contempt. For 18 months, the mobs taunting the troops grew larger, angrier, more daring. In early March 1770, a small group of British soldiers came to blows with a crew of Boston ropemakers. No shots were fired, but several colonists were injured. The fuel and the kindling were now in place. Now, all

Artifact

Britain's foes seized upon the Boston Massacre to inflame the public—the name by which history knows the event is a tribute to the incendiary genius of Samuel Adams. The coffins below, representing four of the five colonial dead, were featured on a broadside published by Paul Revere shortly after the event. Along with newspapers, broadsides—one-off printed sheets tacked up and handed out around the city—were the mass media of the day. The engraving at left, titled *The Bloody Massacre*, accompanied a doggerel verse damning the British:

> Like fierce Barbarians grinning o'er their Prey
> Approve the Carnage and enjoy the Day.

The funeral for the slain men was the largest yet held in North America. More than 10,000 people—two-thirds of the city's population—turned out to rail against British oppression.

Paul Revere's engraving of the event is far from fair and balanced, but it served its purpose as effective political propaganda

the gun barrels and blades, bellowing the word "Fire!" In the confusion, Preston repeatedly ordered, "Don't fire!" Private Hugh Montgomery may only have heard the last word: he raised his musket to eye level and pulled the trigger.

The first colonial to die was Crispus Attucks, a former slave who was half–African American and half–Native American. He had spent 20 years at sea to avoid a return to slavery and was preparing to depart on a voyage to England. Seconds later, three more British troops discharged their weapons and two more colonials fell dead. A third fusillade cut down eight more Americans: two of them died; six survived.

The crowd rapidly dispersed. But the damage was done. Boston's propagandists got busy: Samuel Adams coined the phrase "Boston Massacre," and Paul Revere published an engraving of the scene (*left*) that depicted Crispus Attucks as a white man, shifted the time to mid-afternoon, and added a

beating, fifers playing, colours flying, up King Street." — Paul Revere, 1768

that was needed to ignite serious violence was a spark.

A few days later, on the evening of March 5, a gang of boys approached British troops outside their barracks on King Street (now State Street), near the Customs House. A scuffle ensued—which side incited the other will forever remain in dispute. Tempers flared, voices rose, and soon church bells rang, a signal for the citizenry to assemble. As the crowd swelled, slurs were hurled at the now frightened soldiers—then snowballs, then pieces of ice, then rocks and clubs.

An officer, Captain John Preston, appeared on the scene and attempted to calm the crowd, agitating them further. The men at the front of the mob closed in on the soldiers, shouting, "Fire and be damned, we know you dare not!" As the infantrymen fixed their bayonets and loaded their muskets, the men at the front rank of the crowd pressed their chests against

sarcastic sign reading BUTCHER'S HALL to the Customs House.

The colonists wouldn't know it for weeks, but amid these incendiary events the British Parliament had, that very day, repealed the hated Townshend Acts. The following November, the British troops involved in the incident were brought to trial for murder. The chief counsel for the defense—gutsily defying public opinion—was contrarian lawyer John Adams. In a mighty victory for the rule of law in America, Adams convinced a jury of colonists that the soldiers had acted in reasonable fear of their lives. All were acquitted, except for two privates, who were branded and expelled from the Army.

The colonial relationship was now in tatters. In the wake of the events in Boston, American colonists had more reason than ever to believe they could now deal with the English "bully" as equals—or even sever the ties that bound them. ∎

A First Taste of Rebellion

Samuel Adams, a master of propaganda and protest, stirs up the **Boston Tea Party,** and Britain's harsh response unites the colonies

A contemporary drawing of the Tea Party. When the "Indians" accidentally broke a padlock on one ship, they quickly reimbursed the captain

"If [Governor] Hutchinson will not send tea back to England, perhaps we can

AMERICA'S MOST FAMOUS TEA PARTY was a topsy-turvy affair: Bostonians got themselves into hot water by throwing tea leaves into cold water, though the process certainly involved letting off steam. The ruckus began when Parliament passed a Tea Act in 1773 in hopes of compelling the colonies to purchase tea directly from Britain's foundering East India Company rather than from colonial importers, who often sold smuggled tea from Holland. The new law was seen by Americans as an attempt to undercut local merchants in order to reward a London monopoly, and a boycott soon spread across the colonies. But a boycott was far too passive a strategy for Boston's brilliant rebel, Samuel Adams.

On Dec. 16, 1773, Adams presided over a raucous meeting sponsored by the Sons of Liberty at Boston's Old South Church. A crowd of more than 8,000 people filled the hall and spilled into the streets outside. Adams, who was growing increasingly adept at whipping mobs into a frenzy, urged the crowd to defy the British by tossing the officially sanctioned tea into the harbor.

On a cue from Adams, several dozen Sons of Liberty emerged from the back of the church costumed as Mohawk Indians. They led the whooping crowd to the wharf, where H.M.S. *Dartmouth, Eleanor* and *Beaver* were tied up, laden with East India Company tea, then boarded the vessels and began hurling 342 cases of tea overboard.

Adams was resolved to score a political victory without provoking a bloody crackdown. He admonished the rebels, "No violence, or you'll hurt the cause!" Nor were the Americans the only ones practicing a studied restraint. As one patriot recalled, "We were surrounded by British armed ships, but no attempt was made to resist us."

The spectacular piece of political theater electrified the colonies. Parliament retaliated by passing five laws Americans soon branded the Intolerable Acts, which closed Boston Harbor, established martial law and effectively abolished local government in Massachusetts. Though the acts only affected Massachusetts, their severity united colonials everywhere, who now began organizing a Continental Congress. After hearing of the events in Boston, King George III predicted, "The die is now cast. The Colonies must either submit or triumph." Far be it from us to argue with a King. ∎

brew a pot of it especially for him!" — Samuel Adams, Dec. 16, 1773

In this 1857 painting, William Walcutt imagines New Yorkers tearing down the statue of King George III at Bowling Green in Manhattan

An Intellectual Revolution

The Age of Enlightenment stirs up radical ideas about man's place in society, giving birth to a liberating new proposition: **the Rights of Man**

IMAGINE A WELL-REASONED ARGUMENT AGAINST FAMILY, free speech, the ownership of private property and any other values you believe to be right and just—and you will have some idea of how radical the statement "All men are created equal" sounded to 18th century ears. We are taught to think of the American Revolution as a political revolt that led to an outright war. Such uprisings would never have begun, much less succeeded, had they not been sparked by an intellectual insurrection that lit fires around the world in the mid-1700s and continues to burn to this day.

Europeans of the 1700s thought of themselves as, above all else, supremely modern. They had achieved advances in science and culture that would have been unimaginable to their forebears of only a few generations earlier. All this progress, it was believed, rested upon a hard-won recognition of the natural order of things: God, who had created the world, selected the ablest and worthiest men to govern it as kings, while everyone else accepted their divinely ordained stations in this life and worked humbly for reward in the next. This social hierarchy was mirrored by a religious hierarchy that answered the needs of the soul. Acceptance of this order distinguished humans from animals and made it possible to know the mind of God by unlocking secrets like the movement of the planets. But rejecting this order (as the American colonists are doing in the illustration above) threatened to return humanity to chaos and squalor of the Dark Ages.

"The art of government is to make two-thirds of the people pay all it

In fact, the revolutions in science were being paced, if more slowly, by an evolution in politics. Beginning with the Magna Carta, the 1215 document in which English nobles forced King John to relinquish his claims to absolute rule, and progressing through Britain's 1689 Bill of Rights (in which Parliament asserted, among other things, the freedom of British subjects to bear arms, petition the King, elect their own representatives and refuse to pay taxes to which those representatives had not consented), power was slowly but inexorably trickling down to ever larger numbers of people.

As these two forces had converged, the skeptical inquiry that was driving scientists spilled over into politics, and the dam broke. In 1690, the British philosopher John Locke (from whom Jefferson would later borrow so freely that he was sometimes accused of plagiarism) would write in his *Second Treatise on Civil Government* about the universal right to "life, liberty and property." In 1748, the French scholar Montesquieu wrote in *The Spirit of Laws* that governmental power ought to be divided between those who make laws (the legislature), those who enforce them (the executive) and those who interpret them (judges)—and that these three branches should be independent of one another. By 1762, French philosopher Jean-Jacques Rousseau, in his *Social Contract*, was insisting that governments derive their powers from the consent of the people they govern.

In Europe, these musings were, at least for the first half of the 18th century, largely theoretical. The weight of law, tradition and all the armed power of established states rendered such heresies harmless. But in Britain's American colonies, the situation was very different. Here, a confident, self-reliant population led by a well-educated, affluent élite was poised to exploit the opportunities offered by a vast wilderness they had scarcely begun to explore, at precisely the moment when Enlightenment thinking was reaching full flower. It is difficult to imagine a more fertile breeding ground for what followed.

When the great French skeptic Voltaire embraced Ben Franklin in Paris in 1778, they were hailed as twin prophets of a new age of reason. Indeed, only six years after the end of the American Revolution, an uprising that drew inspiration both from Enlightenment thinkers and from

Voltaire
Locke

Men like Thomas Jefferson, Ben Franklin and others who valued reason more highly than tradition threatened civilization itself: suggesting that princes and peasants were equal in the eyes of God meant that the traditional mediators between heaven and earth, kings and priests, were suddenly far less important, perhaps entirely obsolete. If all men are "endowed by their creator" with certain inalienable rights (rather than granted rights by their King), they would have little need for middlemen in robes (royal or clerical) to administer those rights.

Inspired by radical advances in science and "natural philosophy" pioneered by Isaac Newton, René Descartes and Michel de Montaigne in the 16th and 17th centuries, thinkers of the Enlightenment were predisposed to question everything. But there were, at first, strict limits on the sedition of scholars: suggesting that the earth moved around the sun might no longer get you burned at the stake, but implying that the King was not anointed by God could still cost you your head.

the U.S. example but that followed a very different course, took place in Voltaire's France, which adopted the Declaration of the Rights of Man in 1789. Even Britain began hewing to the U.S. course, continuing its steady march toward increasing individual freedoms.

In the minds of America's Founding Fathers, the demarcation between the revolution of ideas they fomented and the battlefield victory that followed remained distinct. As John Adams would write to Thomas Jefferson in 1815, "the War ... was no part of the Revolution. It was only an effect and consequence of it. The Revolution was in the minds of the people, and this was effected ... years before a drop of blood was drawn at Lexington." ∎

possibly can for the benefit of the other third." —Voltaire

Across the Great Divide

A crazy quilt of very dissimilar settlements—the American colonies—discover there is strength in unity at the **First Continental Congress**

IN 1765, FACED WITH THE STAMP ACT, WHICH THREATENED TO cripple their commerce, colonials banded together to form the Stamp Act Congress. This body coordinated boycotts and sent to London a single petition that spoke for most of the colonies, but it was seen as a temporary solution to a passing crisis. For the next nine years the colonies did not work together, though their legislatures and assemblies discussed common interests through committees of correspondence, first established by Virginia's House of Burgesses. Now, shocked into action by the harsh Intolerable Acts imposed by Parliament after the Boston Tea Party, Americans re-solved to come together, right now. In September 1774, 55 delegates from 12 of the 13 colonies convened in Philadelphia. Georgia declined to attend: the newest and most distant colony, it desperately needed Crown support in its ongoing battles with the Creek Indians.

"The members met at the City Tavern, at 10 o'clock," John Adams wrote later, "and walked to the Carpenters' Hall, where they took a view of the room, and of the chamber where is an excellent library." The delegates approved the space—except for those from Pennsylvania and New York, who also took a contrarian stand on a far more compelling matter. They were

"On the fortitude, on the wisdom and on the exertions of this important day, under strict instructions to seek a compromise that would avoid the break with Britain that some of the more radical participants, mostly from New England, were openly espousing.

After electing Virginian Peyton Randolph to serve as their president, the delegates began debating plans to shake off the yoke of the Intolerable Acts. Joseph Galloway of the Pennsylvania delegation proposed "A Plan of Union of Great Britain and the Colonies," which would have answered those whose rallying cry was "No taxation without representation," and would also strengthen America's ties to England rather than sever them. The plan called for a new Colonial Parliament under a President General appointed by the King; on matters relating to the colonies, the British and American parliaments would each have veto power over the other's actions.

After weeks of debate the Pennsylvania plan was close to passage, but it was scotched by that minatory man from Massachusetts, Paul Revere, who galloped into Philadelphia clutching the Suffolk Resolves, a set of resolutions passed by citizens of Suffolk County that detailed the hardships afflicting Massachusetts under the Intolerable Acts and called for stronger action against Britain. Galloway's plan was narrowly defeated, with the opposition led by the Massachusetts and Virginia delegations, a potent pairing that included northern cousins John and Samuel Adams and southern squires George Washington, Richard Henry Lee and Patrick Henry.

Instead, the Congress ratified the "Declaration of Rights and Grievances," a document addressed to King George that asserted the legal sanctity of "life, liberty, and property" for the American colonists and asked him to rescind the Intolerable Acts. A few days later, the delegates approved the creation of a Continental Association to halt trade between the colonies and England on Dec. 1, 1774, if the Intolerable Acts were not repealed by that date. In a less trumpeted move, the delegates also voted to advise the assemblies of each colony that if the Intolerable Acts remained in effect, its citizens should raise a militia and prepare for war. ■

Chaplain Jacob Duché leads the delegates in prayer, as imagined by a 19th century artist

is suspended the fate of this new world." —The Suffolk Resolves, 1774

Forced March to Sunset

Migrating ever westward as the British and colonials clear their lands, America's native peoples unite in a desperate revolt, **Pontiac's Rebellion**

DOES THIS STORY SOUND FAMILIAR? AS TROUBLED TIMES beset a community, a self-styled prophet emerges, predicting the end of the world and calling for repentance and a return to more traditional ways. And Neolin, a Native American mystic who foretold the end of the world in the 1760s, was right: his world, and the world of all the Indian tribes that were being gradually overwhelmed by a steady influx of British colonists, was doomed.

In the 150 years since British settlers began landing on the East Coast of North America, their relations with the native inhabitants had followed a predictable, deadly pattern: initial friendship when the colonists were needy; growing distrust of the Indians as the colonies became self-reliant; outright hatred and warfare as the colonies expanded and the two peoples battled for living room along the frontier. Meanwhile, Indians perished by the tens of thousands from European diseases, against which the tribes had no immunity.

For almost two centuries the Native Americans migrated westward, surrendering land from the Atlantic Coast to the Alleghenies, then to the western Appalachians, at last finding themselves with their backs against the Mississippi River. The pace of retreat slowed somewhat by the mid-1700s, as British westward expansion was blocked by the French territory of Louisiana, and the French seemed content to trade with the Indian tribes of the Ohio Valley, rather than conquer them. But in 1763, when the British came into possession of all France's holdings in North America at the conclusion of the French and Indian War, this temporary truce came to an end.

From the start, British policy seemed calculated to offend the tribes. The British abandoned the practice of making annual gifts to the chiefs, but the Indians had come to depend

Pontiac

Before the words of the Delaware Prophet set his heart on fire, Pontiac was an unremarkable prince who seemed destined to preside over serene prosperity. In the Algonquin language, the word *ottawa* means "trader," and the Ottawa tribe had been known for centuries among Native Americans for intertribal commerce. Born around 1720, Pontiac assumed the leadership of the Ottawa nation in 1755; his English name is a corruption of his real name, Obwandiyag.

Ongoing British and colonial encroachment upon his tribe's land and trade drove Pontiac slowly in the direction of war. But when he signed the peace treaty ending that war in 1766, Pontiac said to his former enemies, "I speak in the name of all the Nations to the westward whom I command: it is the will of the Great Spirit that we should meet here today, and before him and all present I take you by the hand and never will part with it." The trader turned warrior was as good as his word: from that day until his murder by a brave of the Peoria tribe in 1769, Pontiac never raised his hand or his voice against the white man again.

"If you are French ... join us. If you are English, we declare war against you.

on the guns and powder, steel axes and fishing nets, along with luxuries like tobacco and liquor, that had been supplied by the French during their decades of co-existence. With their dignity wounded, their livelihoods imperiled and their lands under renewed threat by British expansion—now burgeoning at a pace never envisioned by the French—the tribes of the Ohio Valley and the Great Lakes area convened a council of war on the banks of the Ecorse River near Detroit in April 1763.

Ringing in the ears of the assembled chiefs were the words of Neolin, now remembered as the Delaware Prophet, who quoted a command given to him by the Master of Life in a vision: "Before [the white men] came on your lands, did you not live by bow and arrow? You had no need of gun nor powder … As regards those who have come to trouble your country, drive them out, make war on them! I love them not, they know me not, they are my enemies!" One among the chiefs stood up. Pontiac, chief of the Ottawa tribe and a disciple of Neolin's, roared that "it is important for us, my brothers, that we exterminate from our lands this nation which seeks only to destroy us." A coalition of six nations quickly agreed to follow Pontiac into combat.

After three months of preparation, the warriors of these tribes, eventually numbering more than a dozen nations, marched on the 13 British forts in the Ohio Valley and the western Great Lakes region. Within weeks, 11 of the forts were in Pontiac's hands. But his biggest victory was scored in London, where the British government, its treasury exhaust-

ed, issued the Proclamation of 1763, which forbade further settlement east of the Appalachians. On the battlefield, however, the two forts that mattered most—Fort Pitt in western Pennsylvania and Fort Detroit in modern-day Michigan—held out against prolonged sieges. When the British sent large expeditions to relieve the forts the following spring, Pontiac's warriors stalked the soldiers and fought them—bravely, but vainly. Courage was no match for superior British muskets.

By the closing months of 1764, Pontiac's ammunition was running short. The British cannily negotiated separate peace treaties with several of the confederated tribes and introduced a hideous new tactic, presenting blankets carrying smallpox to the Indians. Both tactics proved effective. In 1765, Pontiac agreed to an honorable peace, in which the nations he led surrendered no territory. For their part, the British decided it was less expensive to trade with the Indians (and supply them with gifts) than it was to fight them. As for the English promise to leave the lands west of the Appalachian range to the Indians, it was kept but not intentionally. By the time white settlers were ready to press westward once again, the British were gone and the U.S. was an independent nation. Sadly, the change in flag brought no change in fortunes for Pontiac and his people: the killing, the deceit and the migrations resumed in earnest, just as Neolin had foretold. ■

Frederick Remington, the noted artist of Western scenes, painted this picture of Pontiac's braves besieging Fort Detroit

Let us have your answer."

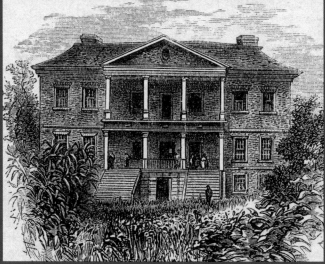

Splendor and Slavery

Framed by Spanish moss dangling from live oaks, Drayton Hall outside Charleston, S.C., epitomizes life in the Southern colonies before the Revolution. Built by wealthy John Drayton beginning in 1738, the mansion was the showplace of a vast plantation that at its height kept some 500 slaves occupied in growing indigo and rice. With most land controlled by a few large plantation owners, a vast gulf opened between rich and poor in the South, and the growing reliance on slaves to work the fields further distinguished the Southern colonies from their Northern neighbors, where a burgeoning middle class helped break down old British social divides. That these diverging colonies would come together in common cause is a testament to the ineptitude of the British, who, with more astute political management, might have successfully driven a wedge between them.

Drayton Hall was a prize for both sides in the Revolution. John Drayton had sent his sons to England to be educated, even to be presented to the King, yet three of four of them enlisted in the local militia after Lexington and Concord. John's oldest son, William Henry Drayton, once a devout Loyalist, was one of the earliest voices for American independence; in his role as president of the South Carolina assembly, he led the cheers when the Declaration of Independence was read aloud under the Liberty Tree in Charleston on Aug. 5, 1776.

In 1779, after the focus of the war shifted to the South, Drayton Hall was looted by British troops as they moved to capture Charleston. John Drayton died as he fled before the British; William Henry Drayton died two months later in Philadelphia, where he was serving as a delegate to the Second Continental Congress. For the next two years, Drayton Hall was headquarters for British forces in the Charleston area. The tables were turned in 1782: after the British surrendered at Yorktown, American General Anthony Wayne moved into the mansion. Ironically, Charles Drayton—who had played both sides of the fence in the Revolution—came into the estate, where he lived until his death in 1820. ■

Drayton Hall

in front, and took the Virginia Reg't. to guard him." —Diary, William McDowell

"The Peculiar Institution"

In rejecting British rule, the colonists declared that all men ought to be free—well, almost all men. How **slavery** became America's original sin

A MODERN-DAY GEORGE WASHINGTON—FORMER GENERAL and Secretary of State Colin Powell—once reflected that "the Declaration of Independence, I think, is one of the most remarkable documents in the world" but went on to lament that "it didn't apply to black folks." The man who wrote that Declaration, with its ringing reveille that "all men are created equal" was one Thomas Jefferson, slaveholder. Monticello's master well understood the inconsistency of his actions, once writing to a friend, "If there is a just God, we are going to pay for this." Americans did pay, and continue to pay, for this system that bound master and slave, white and black, in its iron embrace.

In 1619 a Dutch sea captain bound for the Caribbean put in at Jamestown, Va., where he traded some of his valuable cargo—human beings in shackles—for food and other supplies. Although the transatlantic slave trade had been thriving for nearly a century, almost all its traffic was between Africa and the Spanish colonies of Central and South America. But the Virginia colonists soon realized the value of unpaid labor, and by the next year they were placing orders for more slaves with Dutch, English, Spanish, French and Portuguese shippers. Plantation owners in neighboring colonies, especially Maryland and the Carolinas, quickly followed suit. The influx of low-cost workers made it possible for their vast farms to prosper by exporting shiploads of labor-intensive crops to Europe—first rice, then sugar, coffee, cotton and tobacco.

For the first decade or so of slavery's existence in America, the colonists improvised the legal aspects of the system that came to be called—in a triumph of obfuscation—"the peculiar institution." Most early slaves were considered indentured

An overseer manages two female slaves in this 18th century illustration by Benjamin Latrobe. At far right, a newspaper notice advertises a slave auction on a ship in Charleston, S.C., whose port was shut down owing to a smallpox epidemic

"... so much misery [is] produced by this pestilential detestable traffic in the servants, and a handful were allowed to work their way to freedom. Within 20 years of the 1619 landing, however, the word slave began appearing in colonial records and statutes. By 1640, Maryland had formally changed the legal status of African slaves to that of property. The following year, Massachusetts did the same, describing as legal chattel "such strangers as willingly sell themselves or are sold to us."

While more than 70% of all the slaves brought to America lived and worked in the South, slavery was practiced in every colony. Eleven black slaves were brought to New York (then New Netherland) by the Dutch West India Company only six years after the first group landed at Jamestown; they helped build the defensive barrier from which Wall Street takes its name. New York would be home to the largest number of slaves among the Northern colonies for another 175 years. While northern cities like Boston and New York had less use for unskilled agricultural labor than did Jamestown and Charleston, they grew fat on the trade, their wharves thick with the masts of ships that brought slaves in and crops out.

So lucrative was the market for humans in bondage that slaves came to be known as "black gold" centuries before that term was applied to describe oil. The explosive growth fueled by this boom stoked the demand for more and more unpaid laborers. By the late 1760s, there were between 250,000 and 500,000 black slaves in Britain's American colonies, and slave ships were bringing Africans in chains to the New World at a rate of more than 50,000 new arrivals each year.

As visions of independence began to entice colonial minds, the moral implications of slavery emerged, belatedly, as an inescapable, intractable issue. Passionate advocates of the rights of man denounced the trade; Benjamin Franklin called it "an atrocious debasement of human nature." One eloquent voice against the practice was that of Jefferson, who eventually owned more than 200 slaves. In an early draft of the Declaration of Independence, he ignored colonial complicity in slavery while condemning King George for having "waged cruel war against human nature itself, violating its most sacred rights of life and liberty in the persons of a distant people who never offended him, captivating and carrying them into slavery in another hemisphere or to incur miserable death in their transportation thither."

That passage was struck from the final version of the Declaration, at the insistence of Southern delegates. But the peculiar institution could not be written off so easily: America would pay a grievous price for its original sin. The bill came due in 1861. ■

bodies and souls of men" —Ben Franklin, London *Chronicle*, 1772

"Franklin found electricity a phenomenon, and left it a science."

Go Fry a Kite

Ben Franklin put the American colonies in the forefront of science with his experiments in **electricity**—but did he really fly that famous kite?

IN THE MID–18TH CENTURY, BEN FRANKLIN WAS THE ONLY citizen of the Americas that Europeans knew by name. His celebrity was not the result of his annual publication, *Poor Richard's Almanack;* rather, it rested on his work in science as the world's foremost investigator of electricity. The iconic moment of the Philadelphia polymath's scientific career took place on a storm-tossed June day in 1752, when Franklin, joined by his son William, hoisted a kite with a wire poking out of it high over Philadelphia. As the skies darkened, the kite's hemp string bristled with electricity, like a cat's fur after being stroked. Franklin brought his knuckles close to a brass key dangling from the end of the string. A spark leaped through the air, giving him a powerful jolt—and immeasurable pleasure. No longer could anyone doubt that the small electrical charges created in the era's popular parlor games and the Jovian bolts thundering from the heavens were one and the same.

And yet … is this oft-told tale another Founders myth, like Washington's confessing to axing his father's cherry tree? In his book *Bolt of Fate* (2003; Public Affairs Press), Tom Tucker calls the whole thing a hoax, echoing the spoofs Franklin confected for his almanac. But Tucker's evidence is slim. He makes much of the improbability of flying a kite weighted down by a heavy key, ignoring Franklin's long history of kite flying, and of his delay in publicizing the experiment, although only three months elapsed from event to publication. More to the point, scientific fraud seems wildly out of character for Franklin. As Harvard chemist and Franklin buff Dudley Herschbach, a Nobel laureate, notes, "It would have been utterly inconsistent with all of his other work in [science] for him to claim he'd done something he had not."

Most scholars agree Franklin flew the kite, but the larger point is the impact of his work. When he caught the electricity bug in his 40s, "electrick fire" was a playful if puzzling amusement. His experiments led him to startlingly modern conclusions. The "fire," he said, is a single "fluid," not the dual "vitreous" and "resinous" electricities postulated by European savants. It exists in two states: plus and minus (terms he coined, along with positive and negative, battery and conductor). Furthermore, he said, if there is an excess of charge in one conductor, it must be precisely balanced, as in double-entry bookkeeping, by a deficit in another. Stated another way, electrical charge is always conserved, an important new principle descended from Newton's conservation of momentum. When sparks fly between two charged bodies, Franklin declared, they instantly restore the equilibrium between them.

Franklin wasn't the first to propose a kinship between harmless sparks and a lightning bolt. But he was the first to suggest an experiment to prove it. The Royal Society of London published his proposal, yet it was the French who put it to the test. The experiment, which Franklin first revealed in a letter to his English agent in July 1750, called for installing on a high place, like a steeple, a sentry box with a metal pole extending from its roof. If an electrified storm cloud passed overhead, Franklin said, the pole—preferably sharpened at the end—would pull out a small amount of the cloud's "fire." (In modern terms, it would induce an electrical charge in the pole.) An observer in the sentry box could detect the charge by touching the pole with an insulated ground wire and drawing sparks. Or if the pole itself was grounded, it would extract all the cloud's "fire" in a lightning bolt and sweep it harmlessly into the earth. Franklin had created the lightning rod.

Late in August 1752, Franklin would learn the French had succeeded with his experiment that spring. But he had already set about undertaking it himself in June of that year—with a special wrinkle. The steeple he had hoped to use was unfinished, and he decided he could prove his case just as easily with a wired kite; it would rise even higher in the sky. So why did he do it on the sly? Joseph Priestley, the British chemist and a Franklin crony, later explained, "… dreading the ridicule which too commonly attends unsuccessful attempts in science, he communicated his intended experiment to nobody but his son, who assisted him in raising the kite."

When the secret finally got out, it had sweeping repercussions. Franklin's experiment showed that electricity was not just an amusing "bizarrery" but a force of nature, like gravity. It also illustrated an Enlightenment ideal: that pure science—science done for the sheer joy of exploring nature—could have enormous practical consequences, as shown by the lightning rod. The invention drastically reduced a perennial fire threat to churches and other tall structures. Most profoundly, it shook the belief that lightning was a sign of God's displeasure.

What Franklin modestly described as his "electrical amusements" made him the world's most famous scientist. The German philosopher Immanuel Kant called him the "new Prometheus." Most important, Franklin's fame helped open French hearts—and purse strings—when years later he came calling at Louis XVI's court on behalf of his embattled young nation. As the French financier A.R.J. Turgot would say of the kite flyer from Philadelphia, "He snatched lightning from the sky and the scepter from tyrants." ∎

PHOTO-ILLUSTRATION FOR TIME BY MICHAEL ELINS

—Carl van Doren

HIS LIFE AND WORK

Born in Boston on Jan. 17, 1706

Is apprenticed to his brother James as a printer

Runs away to Philadelphia and takes job as a printer

Opens his own printshop

Publishes the first edition of *Poor Richard's Almanack*

Becomes Philadelphia postmaster

Writes proposal that creates the Philadelphia Academy, later known as the University of Pennsylvania

1710   1720   1730   1740

Where he lived:
- Boston
- Philadelphia
- London
- Paris

Devises swimming fins to make himself go faster in the waters of Boston Harbor

Writes "Silence Dogood" essays

Writes "Busy-Body" essays. Buys the *Pennsylvania Gazette*

Forms the Union Fire Company, a volunteer brigade

Organizes the American Philosophical Society

A Beautiful Mind

For Franklin, bright ideas struck early and often

ELECTRICAL EXPLORATION

LIGHTNING RODS ►

Well before the famous kite experiment, Franklin had speculated that lightning was electricity. His revolutionary idea was to **conduct that electricity safely** into the ground to save buildings from fires. The simple metal rod connected to a wire made Franklin famous throughout Europe and the colonies

◄ OPPOSITES ATTRACT

Starting with a simple glass tube that collected **static charge** when rubbed, above, and later using a hand-cranked machine built for the same purpose, left, Franklin meticulously experimented on the behavior of electricity. Perhaps his most important discovery was that electrical phenomena involve equal amounts of opposite charges. He used the terms **positive** and **negative** to describe them

▼ THE BATTERY

Franklin also discovered the difference between **conductors** and **insulators** of electricity. He used a device called a **Leyden jar** to hold and discharge electricity—even using some to kill a turkey for a feast. Wiring together charged plates, and later jars, he created and named an **electrical battery**

AMERICAN PHILOSOPHICAL SOCIETY

Sources: Franklin Institute Science Museum; American Philosophical Society; Bucks County (Pa.) Historical Society; *Experiments and Observations on Electricity,* by Benjamin Franklin; *The Ingenious Dr. Franklin,* edited by Nathan G. Goodman; *Benjamin Franklin's Science,* by I. Bernard Cohen; "The Myth of the Franklin Stove," by Samuel Edgerton, *Early American Life* magazine, June 1976; *Benjamin Franklin, a Biographical Companion,* by Jennifer L. Durham; *The Papers of Benjamin Franklin,* Yale University Press; *Benjamin Franklin,* by Walter Isaacson

TIME Graphic by Ed Gabel and Jackson Dykman

FRANKLIN INSTITUTE SCIENCE MUSEUM; PHOTOGRAPHS FOR TIME BY TED THAI (4)

Electricity writings published. Elected to Pennsylvania Assembly

Wages press crusade in London on behalf of the colonies. Prints maps showing the Gulf Stream, based on his own temperature readings and observations

Negotiates treaties of alliance and commerce with France

Negotiates, with John Adams and John Jay, peace treaty with Britain

Publishes a paper that, half-joking, advocates shifting the clocks in summer to create daylight saving time

| 1750 | 1760 | 1770 | 1780 | 1790 |

French and Indian War begins. Devises and proposes a plan for a federal union

Assembly passes his bill providing for night watchmen and street lighting. Designs a new type of street lamp

Elected to Second Continental Congress. Proposes the first Articles of Confederation

At Constitutional Convention, formally proposes "great compromise" that creates a House with proportional representation and a Senate with equal votes per state

Dies on April 17, 1790, at age 84

PRACTICAL IMPROVEMENTS

◄ BIFOCALS
Tired of changing eyeglasses to see near and far, Franklin simply combined **two pairs into one.** He praised his device as allowing him to see both his dinner and who was speaking to him across the table

THE LIBRARY COMPANY ►
Books were scarce in 1730s Philadelphia, so Franklin founded America's first **subscription library,** where members paid dues for the privilege of borrowing books. The organization survives to this day

◄ ODOMETER
As postmaster of the colonies, Franklin used this device to count the **revolutions of wagon wheels** to calculate the most efficient mail routes

THE PENNSYLVANIAN FIREPLACE ►
Franklin had nothing to do with the **potbellied stove** known by his name today. Rather, his invention was a complicated—and ultimately unsuccessful—device intended to force heat into a room while carrying smoke away. But installing the stove meant **rebuilding an entire fireplace,** and the device apparently couldn't generate enough air flow to force the smoke out. Nevertheless, Franklin's invention was an important stepping-stone in the development of more efficient home heating

Side vents release convected heat

Iron surfaces radiate heat

Rising smoke has to be forced downward before reaching the chimney

Cold air enters from the cellar

AMUSEMENTS

ARMONICA ►
Inspired by a man who played melodies by rubbing his wet fingers around the rims of wine glasses, Franklin built a machine to mimic the process. The player spun **glass bowls**— different sizes for each note—on a spindle and pressed wetted fingers to the glass to play tunes

▼ MAGIC SQUARES
Franklin enjoyed creating "arithmetical curiosities" in which lines have the same sum vertically, horizontally and when "bent" (in this case, 260)

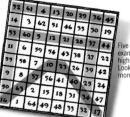

Five examples highlighted. Look for more.

Volunteer colonial militia—Minute-men—drill in preparation for combat

Marching to War

Revolution: 1775-83

April 1775
Minutemen battle British at Lexington and Concord, Mass.

May 1775
Colonials capture Fort Ticonderoga, N.Y.; Second Continental Congress meets

June 1775
Battle of Bunker Hill, Boston

Winter 1775-76
Failed invasion of Canada by colonies

March 1776
British evacuate Boston

July 1776
Declaration of Independence approved

August 1776
Battle of Long Island, N.Y.; Washington retreats from Brooklyn and Manhattan

December 1776
Washington crosses Delaware, defeats Hessians in surprise attack

January 1777
U.S. recovers New Jersey; British retreat to New York City

September 1777
British occupy Philadelphia

October 1777
Britain's General John Burgoyne surrenders at Saratoga, N.Y.

June 1778
Battle of Monmouth, N.J., a draw; George R. Clark captures Kaskaskia in West

December 1778
British open Southern front at Savannah, Ga.

December 1779
British begin six-month seige of Charleston, S.C.

October 1781
General Charles Cornwallis surrenders at Yorktown, Va.

September 1783
Treaty of Paris technically ends war

Learning in the Saddle

ABATTLEFIELD IS A DANGEROUS PLACE FOR A general to learn his trade, but when George Washington assumed command of the fledgling Continental Army in July 1775, at the request of the Second Continental Congress, on-the-job training was all he had time for. The Virginian, now 43, was unschooled as a tactician—as he had proved when he botched two battles as a very young commander of the Virginia militia near the Forks of the Ohio in the 1750s. But Washington's five years of service in the frontier wars made him the obvious choice to lead the colonial army two decades later. He learned fast: after some grave mistakes early in his command, he marshaled his enormous energy, tactical decisiveness and inspiring presence to become an assured, successful leader.

Washington's best modern biographer, James Thomas Flexner, asserts, "Washington was never really a soldier. He was a civilian in arms." Flexner presents Washington as a political leader who viewed the war more as a struggle to win the hearts and minds of rebel colonists than as an attempt to defeat the British in direct battle. If that language sounds familiar: yes, Washington was not unlike General Vo Nguyen Giap of North Vietnam, another colonial who bedeviled the disciplined armies of distant, far stronger imperial foes with the strategies of modern-day guerrilla warfare.

Early in his command, on the dark night of March 4, 1776, Washington led 3,000 American troops in a stealthy nighttime advance onto the peninsula of Dorchester Neck just outside Boston; when the British awoke the next morning, they found that the colonials commanded a high, fortified ground from whose heights cannons could barrage the city; six days later, the British withdrew. Yet Washington failed to grasp the obvious lesson: when he attempted to fight the British on their own terms, he was often routed.

The turning point for Washington was his brilliant holiday gambit in New Jersey in 1776-77, when, as in Boston, he used his troops' mobility and individual initiative to surprise Britain's Hessian mercenaries at Trenton, then marched his men at double time to Princeton to overwhelm a stunned British garrison. Striking quickly, then melting away, living off the land and the contributions of sympathetic locals, Washington and his men created a new kind of warfare that turned the contest into a battle of attrition that Britain, at an ocean's length from the battlefields, couldn't win. ∎

"... the resources of Britain were inexhaustible ... her fleets covered the ocean ...

Washington in 1781,
as imagined in an 1825 painting
by Rembrandt Peale

General George Washington

we had no preparation ... The sword was to be forged on the anvil of necessity."

John Adams

"I am determined to preserve my independence, even at the expense of my ambition."

The Revolution's Utility Man

HIS ACHIEVEMENTS ARE MONUMENTAL, BUT TO THE HOR-
ror of his admirers, there is no John Adams Monument n
the nation's capital. Perhaps it's because he was the all-purpose
man of the Revolution, whose broad achievements aren't tied
to a specific event. In typical fashion, he led the committee that
drafted the Declaration of Independence, but as he later complained, "Jefferson ran away with ... all the glory of it."

A brilliant, sawed-off, full-of-himself, argumentative pep-
per pot of a man, Adams was one of the great architects of liberty. The Harvard graduate first showed his strong moral fiber
as a young Massachusetts lawyer, defending the hated British
troops who fired on hectoring colonials at the Boston Massacre; in a triumph of advocacy, he won acquittal for all but
two of them. He was a tireless, eloquent delegate at both the
Continental Congresses, chairing no fewer than 25 committees in the second of them. In a great unifying gesture, he proposed a Virginian, George Washington, to lead the colonial
army at a time when the fighting was confined to the North.
He spent much of the Revolutionary War period abroad, serving as an American envoy to France, Holland and Britain; it was
Adams, Ben Franklin and John Jay who won major concessions
from the British in the Treaty of Paris that ended the war.

Adams toiled as the nation's first Vice President (he called
it "the most insignificant office that ever man contrived ... ")
for eight long years, then, in 1797, took on the impossible task
of following the idolized Washington as President. His single
term was a failure; the impolitic Adams rammed the ill-
conceived Alien and Sedition Acts through Congress, and most
Americans denounced as cowardly his real achievement in
avoiding a war with France. Through it all, Adams relied on the
counsel of his wife Abigail to sustain him; they formed one of
the great marital partnerships in U.S. political history. ∎

Vox Populi

Y OU SAY YOU WANT A REVOLUTION? THEN GET yourself a front man, a rock star and phrase-maker who can shake, rattle and roll the masses with a few well-chosen words: a Trotsky or a Che, a John Lennon—or a Thomas Paine. Seldom have a man and a moment collided with such impact as when Paine published *Common Sense* in January 1776. The slim pamphlet seemed to draw in all the vague currents that were floating through colonial minds and crystallize them into sharp weapons, words whose very utterance could cleave the shackles from men's souls: "Of more worth is one honest man to society and in the sight of God, than all the crowned ruffians that ever lived ... Society in every state is a bless-ing, but government even in its best state is but a necessary evil."

We demand that rock stars lead lives of loud desperation, and Paine complied. His failures in life were both many and varied; when he left England to come to America in 1774, he had been a sailor, corsetmaker, teacher, tobacconist and grocer—without success. He arrived in the Philadelphia bearing letters of introduction from Ben Franklin, whom he'd met and impressed in London. Dr. Benjamin Rush, Franklin's ally, urged Paine to put his radical views on monar-chy and liberty into print, and when Paine pub-lished *Common Sense*, its 47 pages raced through the colonies like an intellectual flu. Paine de-nounced monarchy, celebrated the common man, glorified reason and laid the groundwork for the Declaration of Independence. And he wasn't finished: *The American Crisis*, his series of tracts during the Revolutionary War—"These are the times that try men's souls"—continued to inspire the rebels while providing an intellectu-al underpinning for their deeds.

Paine lived fast but failed to die young. His lat-er history is a sad tale; even Americans desert-ed him when he attacked organized religion in *The Age of Reason* (1794-96). No matter: *Com-mon Sense* is news that stays news. ∎

Thomas Paine

"There is another and great distinction for which no truly natural or religious reason can be assigned, and that is the distinction of men into Kings and Subjects."

Paul Revere

"I proceeded to Lexington, through Mistick, and alarmed Mr. Adams and Colonel Hancock"

Cassandra on Horseback

WHEN JOHN SINGLETON COPLEY PAINTED PAUL REVERE IN 1768, the Boston silversmith chose to pose without his jacket, a shocking breach of portrait decorum. The son of a French immigrant, Apollos Rivoire (who Anglicized his name on coming to America), Paul Revere was a proud artisan, a silversmith who also practiced dentistry, crafted surgical tools and produced copper engravings; he wanted to be seen as a hands-on workman rather than a formal gentleman. The early patriot and member of the Sons of Liberty may also have wanted to show off his shirt of linen; it was made in America, defying a British mandate that only linen of English manufacture could be worn in the colonies. The teapot is an emblem of Revere's craftsmanship, not a nod to the Boston Tea Party; the silversmith indeed was one of the leaders of the "In-

dians" that night—five years after this portrait was painted.

Revere was one of a kind, but his famous "midnight ride" of April 18, 1775, was not; it was one of several notable horseback journeys he made in the cause of freedom. A messenger for the Massachusetts Committee of Safety, Revere rode to Philadelphia in September 1774, where his appearance at the First Continental Congress altered the course of the debate. Three months later he rode to Portsmouth, N.H., to alert locals to a potential British landing. On April 16, 1775, he rode to Concord to warn the local militia to move its supply of armaments in case of a British advance; two days later, he set off, as did William Dawes, to warn that the advance was at hand. But he never cried, "The British are coming!" Like other Bostonians, he still regarded himself as a British citizen. ∎

Molly Pitcher

"A cannon shot from the enemy passed directly between her legs" —Joseph P. Martin

BETTMANN CORBIS (AFTER A PAINTING BY C.Y. TURNER)

Woman Warrior

H ER NAME IS GENERIC—IT'S AN 18TH CENTURY TERM FOR A female camp follower who brought water to the troops. Mary Ludwig Hays McCauley, the most famous of "Molly Pitchers" in the Revolutionary War, earned the nickname when she accompanied her husband to the front—in this case, to the Battle of Monmouth in New Jersey in June 1778.

The daughter of a Pennsylvania dairy farmer, Mary had married William Hays, a barber, at age 13. When the firing began, she carried water to her husband's artillery team. The story goes that in the heat of the battle, she joined the men in loading and firing the cannons. Nor is the story legend; it is based on the diary of Joseph P. Martin of Connecticut, who saw her in ac-

tion. His account bears the unmistakable whiff of authenticity: "While in the act of reaching for a cartridge, a cannon shot from the enemy passed directly between her legs without doing any other damage than carrying away all the lower part of her petticoat. Looking at it with apparent unconcern she observed that it was lucky it did not pass a little higher, for in that case it might have carried away something else."

Legend holds that "Molly" was saluted by George Washington himself after the battle; that story bears the unmistakable whiff of iconography. More accurate—and more telling of women's roles in this era—is this fact: after the war, Mary worked as a charwoman at the Pennsylvania State House. ∎

A Judas Among Rebels

IN 1904 WINSTON CHURCHILL WAS DENOUNCED BY HIS FEL-low Conservatives when he bolted from the party to join the Liberals. Twenty years later, he turned his coat again, rejoining the Tories. Denounced as a two-time traitor, he fired back with a memorable riposte: "Anyone can rat," he declared, "but it takes a certain amount of ingenuity to re-rat."

Benedict Arnold is the most famous re-ratter in American history, a man who rebelled against his King, then betrayed his fellow rebels. Arnold, who owned an apothecary in New Haven, Conn., was an early patriot who took up arms after the April 1775 skirmishes at Lexington and Concord and helped Ethan Allen capture Fort Ticonderoga the next month. An impressed George Washington appointed him to head up the invasion of Canada in late 1775. Arnold, a born leader, took 1,000 men on a harrowing march to Quebec City but was defeated in his attempt to take the city's fortress. He stopped the British navy at the Battle of Valcour Island in October 1776; a year later, at the Battle of Saratoga, he rallied the colonial troops and saved the day, although he was not in command.

Arnold was a fighter, not a diplomat; he quarreled with his fellow officers and with the Continental Congress over expenses. Almost crippled at Saratoga, the widower nursed his wounds (and grudges) while wooing Margaret Shippen, a lively young Philadelphia heiress. Their marriage put him in debt, and he turned to shady financial dealings to pay his bills. When Washington put him in charge of the fortress at West Point on the Hudson River, Arnold offered his services to the British for a price. After his scheme to hand over West Point failed, he joined the British in fighting the colonials—ensuring that his name would live in infamy. ∎

Benedict Arnold

"Arnold has betrayed us! Whom can we trust now?" —George Washington, 1780

The Marquis de Lafayette

"When the government violates the people's rights, insurrection is ... the most sacred of the rights and the most indispensable of duties"

The French Connection

THE FRENCH NOBLEMAN ABOVE SEEMS TO BE GAZING RE-flectively into the past—and he probably was. Matthew Harris Jouett painted the Marquis de Lafayette in 1825, when the old veteran received a hero's welcome in America five decades after his grand achievements in the Revolutionary War. Lafayette was a romantic, wealthy aristocrat, orphaned at 13 and not yet 20 when he came to America, seeking glory. As he told the story, he resolved to help the Americans fight the British after dining with an English lord, the Duke of Glou-cester, who expressed his sympathy for the colonial cause.

Lafayette arrived in Philadelphia in the summer of 1777 and presented himself to Congress—which had no idea what to do with him. He was dispatched to General Washington,

who immediately took a liking to the youngster. At the Battle of Brandywine, a disaster for the colonists, Lafayette was wounded, earning the respect of the troops. He weathered Valley Forge, then served with distinction in the 1778 invasion of Canada and in the Monmouth campaign.

In the next few years, Lafayette journeyed between France and the colonies, igniting French fervor for the Americans and the rights of man while forging key links between the two nations that paid off when France sent an expeditionary force to support the colonials. Fittingly, Lafayette was commanding a light division when the timely convergence of French ships and continental armies trapped Cornwallis at Yorktown, seal-ing the Americans' triumph. *Merci, Marquis!*

Revolution's First Skirmish

Marching out of Boston to confiscate rebel guns and arrest Liberty's Sons, the British tangle with Minutemen in the **Battle of Lexington**

I N THE WAKE OF THE HUMILIATING BOSTON TEA PARTY, Britain's King and Parliament resolved to put the lid on the antics of the colonials—by force, if necessary. But for a year and a half, British General Thomas Gage, commander of England's troops in America and military governor of Massachusetts, managed to avoid an explosion. When his troops marched outside the safety of Boston, they were under strict orders not to fire upon the colonial militia units that drilled regularly in most towns and confronted the British with increasing frequency. These detachments trained to be ready for action on a moment's notice; they called themselves "Minutemen." Armed with captured English weapons, they were growing ever bolder in their harassment of Gage's men.

On April 14, 1775, Gage received a communiqué ordering him to confiscate the stockpiles of the local militias and arrest Boston's two most prominent upstarts, John Hancock and Samuel Adams; they would stand trial for high treason.

Gage's spies believed the largest stockpile of rebel weapons in Massachusetts was in Concord, where the Provincial Congress—a new assembly replacing the body banished by the Intolerable Acts—had recently adjourned. The spies also informed him that Adams and Hancock were hiding in the nearby town of Lexington. Both villages were within a day's march of Boston. A single expedition, Gage reasoned, could accomplish two of his most urgent goals in one stroke.

The Sons of Liberty also had spies; they watched closely as a large detachment of British troops was seen assembling late on the night of Tuesday, April 18. Silversmith Paul Revere and a young shoemaker named William Dawes were already standing by; now they set off to warn Adams and Hancock in Lexington and the militia in Concord. Dawes headed south and west; Revere took a shortcut, rowing north across the Charles River to Charlestown, then swinging due west.

When Revere landed at Charlestown and peered back toward Boston, he saw two lights in the tower of the North Church, the signal the British were traveling along Revere's

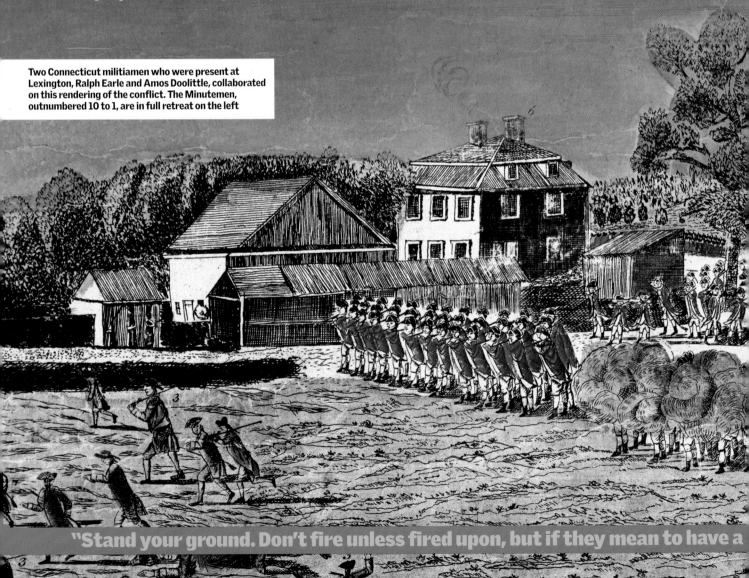

Two Connecticut militiamen who were present at Lexington, Ralph Earle and Amos Doolittle, collaborated on this rendering of the conflict. The Minutemen, outnumbered 10 to 1, are in full retreat on the left

"Stand your ground. Don't fire unless fired upon, but if they mean to have a

"sea route" across the Charles rather than by Dawes' "land route." Just after midnight, Revere borrowed a horse from a Charlestown patriot, Deacon John Larkin, and galloped at full speed for Lexington, sounding the alarm to Minutemen along his path. Church bells were soon piercing the night in Charlestown, Medford and Menotomy.

Arriving at the home of Jonas Clarke in Lexington, where Adams and Hancock were hiding, Revere alerted them. Before dawn, the two men were en route to a safe haven in Philadelphia. Meanwhile, Lexington's Minutemen gathered their weapons and assembled in the center of town. Revere was captured by a squad of British troops as he moved on toward Concord, but he was soon released unharmed.

Seeing lanterns lit up and hearing church bells ring ahead of them, the British realized they had lost the advantage of surprise. Still, they pressed ahead. A few minutes after the sun rose on April 19, 700 British troops approached the Lexington village green. A detachment of some 77 Minutemen were waiting for them, drawn up in a straight line.

"Don't fire unless fired upon," Captain John Parker told his Minutemen as the British approached. Major James Pitcairn gave the same command to the British. Pitcairn then shouted to the colonials, "Disperse, you rebels!" When no one moved, he added, "Damn you, throw down your arms and disperse!"

Seconds later, a single shot rang out; it has never been determined which side fired it. But British muskets echoed that first salvo with several volleys, killing eight Americans and wounding 10 more. Pitcairn's unit, which had taken no casualties, then marched on toward Concord. Before the sun set that day, British troops marched again into Lexington, this time on their way back to Boston from Concord—and Lexington's Minutemen took their revenge. When Pitcairn's unit finally staggered into Boston the next day, 73 of his soldiers were dead, another 26 were missing, and more than 170 were wounded. The conflict that had been simmering since the Tea Party had finally boiled over into outright war. ∎

Artifact

The handbill at right, which lists the names of the American dead in the battles of Lexington and Concord, was published in Boston shortly after the two skirmishes. Local Minutemen were routed at Lexington, but they acquitted themselves better at Concord. By the time the British returned to Boston, 49 Americans had died, and 41 were wounded; at least 73 British were dead, and more than 170 were wounded. Sadly, the memorable quote below is believed to be apocryphal.

war, let it begin here." —Captain John Parker to the Minutemen, April 19, 1775

Old North Bridge

"By the rude bridge that arched the flood ... Here once the embattled farmers

stood/And fired the shot heard round the world." —Ralph Waldo Emerson , 1836

Spanning the Centuries

When the Old North Bridge at Concord, Mass. is seen on a misty day, it's not hard to imagine the events of April 19, 1775—even though we know the structure was rebuilt in 1956. That April morning, after firing the opening volley of what would become the American Revolution, British troops marched past Lexington toward their main objective, the village of Concord. Aware of the earlier action a few miles away, the rebel commander, Colonel James Barrett, was determined not to face the main British force head on; his several hundred Minutemen dug in on a series of ridges overlooking Concord from the west.

When Barrett saw smoke rising from within Concord, he believed that the British were putting the torch to the entire village. (In fact, they were burning small caches of ammunition their search parties had found.) Barrett sent his main force charging toward the North Bridge, now guarded by a small company of English soldiers. When the British fired, killing rebel Captain Isaac Davis, the enraged Americans fought back, and the British retreated into Concord.

Moving quickly now, the Americans charged into Concord. While the British formed up into battle lines, the Minutemen fanned out and fired from behind trees, stone walls and buildings. As militia units from nearby towns began arriving at Concord, the British realized they were surrounded and outnumbered.

As they retreated, the British fought a desperate rearguard action. At every step of their 20-mile journey back to Boston, they faced fire from concealed positions. When the troops finally reached Boston, they found themselves trapped within a city surrounded. The rebels had found something even more powerful: the knowledge that they did not have to fight the British on their own terms. Instead, they could wage war as a swarm of fast-moving individuals, rather than as a fixed phalanx. The emphasis on the individual that was driving the revolution was mirrored in the rebels' military tactics, a declaration of independence in arms. ■

A scene from behind the British lines; Howe's decision to stage a frontal assault proved deadly

ENGRAVING AFTER A PAINTING BY ALONZO CHAPPEL—THE GRANGER COLLECTION, NEW YORK

Bloody Hell on Breed's Hill

In the first major engagement of the war, a poorly organized coalition of New England militias punishes the British at the Battle of Bunker Hill

THE MILITARY ENGAGEMENT AMERICANS CALL THE BATtle of Bunker Hill is one of the Revolution's more ambiguous events. Its name is a misnomer, for it was mainly fought on Breed's Hill, not Bunker Hill. The colonial troops never quite knew who was in command, because two men were. The British plan of battle was utterly wrongheaded. And the fighting ended in a rousing victory—for both sides.

Bunker Hill was fought on June 17, 1775, two months after the skirmishes at Lexington and Concord and five weeks after the stunning rebel victory at Fort Ticonderoga. The colonials were riding high; the Second Continental Congress had begun meeting in Philadelphia on May 10, the day of Ticonderoga's capture. One of its first orders of business was the creation of a Continental Army. Boston was the headquarters of the British military, and New England was the home of the colonies' most active militias, so Congress decided these units would form the nucleus of the new army. To promote colonial

unity, John Adams of Massachusetts proposed George Washington, the Virginia planter who had distinguished himself in the French and Indian War, as commander in chief.

Events were moving swiftly now. Even as Congress was choosing a commander for the war to come, the war was beginning. Militias from around New England were converging on Boston; by the end of May, some 10,000 colonials were encamped around the city, bottling up the 5,000 redcoats within. Britain had already chosen its leaders: on May 25, Generals William Howe, John Burgoyne and Henry Clinton arrived in Boston, joining the continental commander, General Thomas Gage; each of them would play an important role in the conflicts to come. Gage immediately ordered Howe to seize and occupy the Charlestown peninsula, a fist of land jutting out into Boston Harbor; from its high point, atop 110-ft. Bunker Hill, British cannons could command the city across the bay.

The plan seemed likely to succeed—especially to the colonial spies who quickly learned of it. Resolved to stop the British, the colonials decided to take control of the peninsula first. On the evening of June 16, 1,200 Massachusetts and Connecticut troops assembled at Cambridge Common under the command of Colonel William Prescott and Major General Israel Putnam. Both men were veterans of the French and Indian War. Prescott, 49, would lead the Minutemen; Putnam, 57, celebrated for his bravery in Pontiac's Rebellion and other frontier frays, would command the Connecticut militias.

Putnam led the Americans across Charlestown Neck, the thin isthmus of land that connected the peninsula to the mainland. He and Prescott then argued for two hours over which of the two hills on the peninsula to fortify. Military historians agree they made the wrong choice, preferring Breed's Hill, further out on the peninsula, to the higher Bunker Hill, which was closer to the isthmus escape route—and farther from the cannon fire of the British navy.

Just after midnight the rebels began building an earthen redoubt 45 yds. square atop Breed's Hill. When dawn broke, the British were shocked to see the Americans dug in; led by H.M.S. *Lively,* more than half a dozen British ships opened fire on the redoubt, even as the generals began arguing over how to dislodge the rebels. Their decision, often criticized, was not to land behind the Americans, stranding them on the peninsula; it was to land below Breed's Hill and launch a frontal attack on the redoubt. As Howe's 1,500 troops marched up the 62-ft. hill about 2 p.m., the rebels followed Prescott's orders to hold their fire, then opened up with a withering barrage that shattered the British line. The British re-formed, the colonials reloaded, and a second assault was turned back, with severe British losses. After more redcoats landed, the British launched

Eyewitness

In a letter dated June 18, 1775, Abigail Adams describes the battle at Breed's Hill the day after it took place to her husband John, who was in Philadelphia at the time, serving as a delegate to the Second Continental Congress. "The Day, perhaps the decisive Day is come on which the fate of America depends," she begins. She then informs Adams that their close friend Joseph Warren, a physician and a leader among the early patriots, had died in the battle. "The constant roar of the cannon is so [distre]ssing that we can not Eat Drink or Sleep," she continues.

a third, even stronger attack. This time they breached the redoubt, and the colonials, desperately low on ammunition, began a fighting retreat, sustaining their heaviest losses of the day as they fled across Charlestown Neck to the mainland.

Who won? The British occupied the field, but more than a thousand of their men had been wounded, and 226 would die. More than 400 Americans were wounded and 140 died. As the implications of the battle sunk in, though, the Americans realized they had gained more than the British. They had proved they could stand up to British arms, and their gallant stand at Breed's Hill would bring hundreds of new rebels to fight at their side. As for the British, they now knew that they had a serious fight on their hands—a fight in which reinforcements for wounded soldiers were a long ocean voyage away. ∎

Charlestown village, at the foot of Breed's Hill, is ablaze after the British fired carcasses—hollow cannonballs filled with flammable pitch—into its wooden houses

CHARLES TOWN

BOSTON

Fort Ticonderoga

"The first systematical and bloody attempt at Lexington to enslave America

thoroughly electrified my mind." —Ethan Allen

Surprise Attack

Moored in the misty mountains, modern-day Fort Ticonderoga suggests its appearance on May 10, 1775, when rain and fog provided cover for some 400 colonial irregulars approaching the lightly defended British outpost in upstate New York. The fort, built by the French, was strategically located where Lake George and Lake Champlain meet, but what really drew the Americans here was the fort's artillery; desperately short of heavy ordnance, rebel militia leaders realized their only chance of matching the firepower of the British was to capture their weapons.

The expedition was led by Ethan Allen, a 6-ft. frontiersman who led a wild and woolly band of militiamen from the territory that would eventually become Vermont; they called themselves the Green Mountain Boys. Allen shared command with a merchant and militia captain from New Haven, Conn., Benedict Arnold, who arrived as the raid was being organized, bearing a commission from the Massachusetts Committee of Safety to lead the attack. When the Green Mountain Boys refused to serve under Arnold, Allen agreed to share his command. The stealth mission worked flawlessly; the British were outnumbered, and the fort was captured with no serious bloodshed. When the British commander, who was caught with his pants down in the act of dressing, demanded to know under what authority Allen was acting, the mountain man bellowed, "In the name of the Great Jehovah and the Continental Congress!"

Coming just three weeks after the bloody skirmishes at Lexington and Concord, the triumph at Ticonderoga buoyed rebel hearts; more important, the scores of cannon and other artillery pieces captured here would be used months later by George Washington to drive the British from Boston. Sadly, this bracing story isn't all happy; Benedict Arnold went on to command the misbegotten, failed colonial attack on Quebec in the winter of 1775-76, and the British, under General John Burgoyne, recaptured Fort Ticonderoga from the rebels in July 1777. ∎

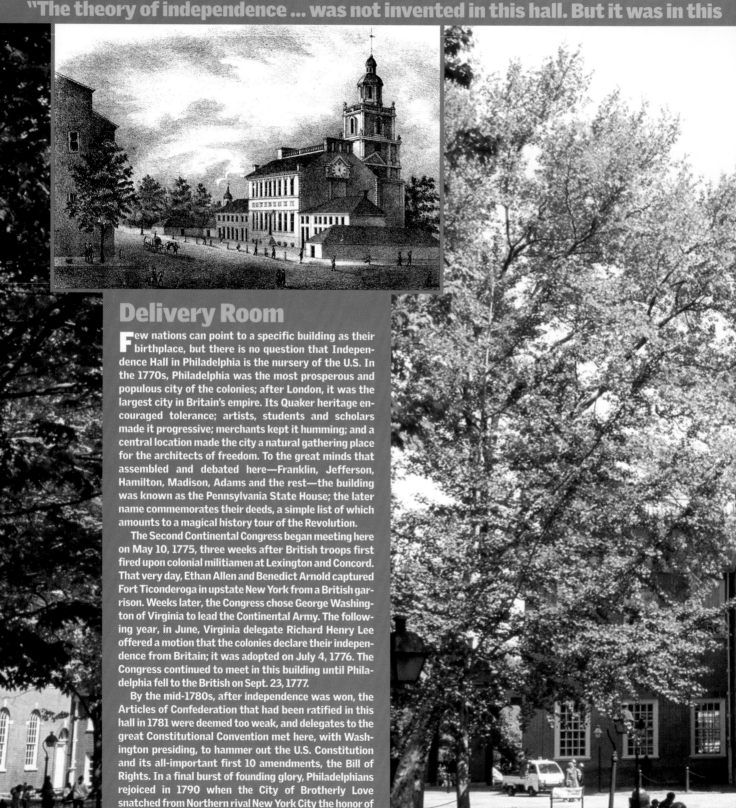

Delivery Room

Few nations can point to a specific building as their birthplace, but there is no question that Independence Hall in Philadelphia is the nursery of the U.S. In the 1770s, Philadelphia was the most prosperous and populous city of the colonies; after London, it was the largest city in Britain's empire. Its Quaker heritage encouraged tolerance; artists, students and scholars made it progressive; merchants kept it humming; and a central location made the city a natural gathering place for the architects of freedom. To the great minds that assembled and debated here—Franklin, Jefferson, Hamilton, Madison, Adams and the rest—the building was known as the Pennsylvania State House; the later name commemorates their deeds, a simple list of which amounts to a magical history tour of the Revolution.

The Second Continental Congress began meeting here on May 10, 1775, three weeks after British troops first fired upon colonial militiamen at Lexington and Concord. That very day, Ethan Allen and Benedict Arnold captured Fort Ticonderoga in upstate New York from a British garrison. Weeks later, the Congress chose George Washington of Virginia to lead the Continental Army. The following year, in June, Virginia delegate Richard Henry Lee offered a motion that the colonies declare their independence from Britain; it was adopted on July 4, 1776. The Congress continued to meet in this building until Philadelphia fell to the British on Sept. 23, 1777.

By the mid-1780s, after independence was won, the Articles of Confederation that had been ratified in this hall in 1781 were deemed too weak, and delegates to the great Constitutional Convention met here, with Washington presiding, to hammer out the U.S. Constitution and its all-important first 10 amendments, the Bill of Rights. In a final burst of founding glory, Philadelphians rejoiced in 1790 when the City of Brotherly Love snatched from Northern rival New York City the honor of being the nation's temporary capital, a distinction it held until the Federal Government moved to its new location in the District of Columbia in 1800. ▪

Independence Hall

hall that the theory became a practice." —John F. Kennedy, 1962

McLEAN COUNTY UNIT #5
105 CARLOCK

Benjamin Franklin altered Jefferson's words on this original manuscript

America's Birth Certificate

Crafted in haste amid the fog of war, **the Declaration of Independence** remains one of the great transforming documents in human history

I**N THE FIRST MONTHS OF 1776, A COURSE ONCE ESPOUSED** by only the most radical of Americans began to seem like common sense to more and more of them: the colonies must declare their independence from Britain. It was, in fact, *Common Sense* that helped turn the tide of public opinion: Thomas Paine's incisive rallying cry, published in January, laid out the case for America's independence from Britain and its monarchy so convincingly that it rallied tens of thousands of Americans to the cause.

Delegates to the Second Continental Congress, assembled in Philadelphia, commonly referred to an entity they called "the United Colonies." Every day brought fresh reasons for

colonial unity—and colonial independence. Congress was already supporting George Washington's Continental Army; that army must be paid, taxes must be levied to support it, and currencies must be regulated to aid tax collection. Nor could America beat the British alone. If the war were to succeed, the colonies would need the assistance of European powers opposed to Britain; ambassadors must be named. In short, an independent colonial government must be formed.

The Congress had tried to reason with King George, had even extended a plea for negotiation, the Olive Branch Petition, in the summer of 1775. That November they learned the King had refused to receive it, an affront that destroyed the position of American moderates. Then, in the spring of '76, after Washington succeeded in driving the British out of Boston, news reached the colonies that a great British invasion force was being assembled, one that would seek to squash the incipient revolution with the aid of hired Hessian mercenaries from Germany and Highland troops from Scotland.

The time for petitions was over; the time for declarations had come. In a matter of months, the once radical faction supporting independence in the Congress had become a majority, spurred on by the assemblies of several colonies, which began writing constitutions of their own, proclaiming their freedom from British authority.

On June 7, Richard Henry Lee of Virginia offered a motion in Congress: "That these United Colonies are, and of right ought to be, free and independent States, that they are absolved from all allegiance to the British Crown, and that all political connection between them and the State of Great Britain is, and ought to be, totally dissolved." Congress debated the issue, with delegates from the "middle states"—Delaware, Pennsylvania and Maryland—being least in favor of independence. A vote on the motion was postponed until July 1, but a committee was chosen to prepare a document laying out the colonial position; it included Ben Franklin, Thomas Jefferson and John Adams.

Jefferson, then only 33, drafted the document on a small lap desk of his own design, while sitting alone in a second-floor room of a home on Market Street in Philadelphia, just a block from Franklin's house. His draft contained a highly specific bill of particulars against the British and chronicled the details of America's failed attempts at conciliation. His words echoed both the language and grand theories of English and Scottish Enlightenment thinkers, most notably the concept of natural rights propounded by John Locke, who saw society as a contract between government and the governed that was founded on the consent of the people.

"Jefferson wrote the magic words of American history, the 55 words in the Declaration that begin 'We hold these truths to be self-evident, that all men are created equal,'" says his biographer Joseph Ellis, a professor of history at Mount Holyoke College and the author of *Founding Brothers*. "That promise and those words are probably the most important words in American history—and possibly all of modern history."

Those words continue to inspire freedom-loving people everywhere; but first, they inspired the delegates in Philadelphia. When debate resumed in Congress on July 1, there was a large majority for independence; on July 2 Lee's motion passed; on July 4 it was

Artifact

This inkstand was used by delegates in signing the Declaration on Aug. 2, 1776. Six weeks before, in late June, Jefferson sent his "rough draft" to Franklin, inviting his comments. Franklin crossed out the last three words of Jefferson's phrase "We hold these truths to be sacred and undeniable" and changed them to the words now enshrined in history: "We hold these truths to be self-evident." By using the word sacred, Jefferson had implied that the equality of men and their endowment by their creator with inalienable rights were an assertion of religion; Franklin's edit turned it into an assertion of rationality. Later, Congress further edited the draft. "I was sitting by Dr. Franklin," Jefferson later recalled, "who perceived that I was not insensible to these mutilations."

adopted; on July 8 it was first read publicly in the streets of Philadelphia, accompanied by the tolling of the Liberty Bell. The great bell cracked, never to ring again: a good omen, Americans hoped.

At the official signing of the parchment copy on Aug. 2, John Hancock, president of the Congress, penned his name with his famous flourish. "There must be no pulling different ways," he declared. "We must all hang together." According to the early American historian Jared Sparks, Franklin replied, "Yes, we must indeed all hang together, or most assuredly we shall all hang separately." Their lives, as well as their sacred honor, were now on the line. ∎

In J.L.G. Ferris' fanciful early 20th century painting, Jefferson (standing), Franklin and John Adams struggle to draft the document

rang all day and almost all night." —John Adams, July 9, 1776

The Empire Strikes Back

Britain mounts a massive amphibious invasion, whips the colonials in the Battle of Long Island, and forces Washington to evacuate New York City

ON JULY 12, 1776, LORD RICHARD HOWE, THE ADMIRAL brother of General William Howe, sailed into Sandy Hook, a finger of New Jersey near Staten Island, in command of 150 ships and fresh troops from Britain. He was joining forces with his brother, Britain's new top continental commander, who had arrived from Nova Scotia in late June with a force that included 130 vessels and 9,300 troops. By late August, 32,000 troops had assembled on Staten Island, one of the largest amphibious forces the British Empire had ever mustered. Britain was through toying with its rebel colonies; it was now prepared to devote the full strength of its mighty military machine to their conquest and domination.

After their defeat at Bunker Hill, the British had holed up in Boston, surrounded by colonial troops and harassed by the populace—until George Washington, now in full command of the Continental Army, executed his first coup of the conflict. Marshaling some 60 British cannons and artillery pieces that had been captured at Ticonderoga and hauled to Boston on a rugged 300-mile journey, he dug them in on the Dorchester Heights overlooking the city on the night of March 6, 1776. That was the last straw for the British. On March 26, General

Howe evacuated his troops from Boston; they sailed from the hotbed of rebellion to Halifax, Nova Scotia.

In the months that followed, Howe refined his plan to invade the colonies and deal the Continental Army a death blow. His target: New York City, a mercantile center that boasted far more British Loyalists than did Boston. The city controlled access up the Hudson River, artery to the continent's interior. If the British could control New York Harbor and the Hudson, they could cleave New England from the southern colonies, then squeeze the region into submission.

Congress, well aware of the plan, urged Washington to defend the port city. The general—who had yet to fight a major en-

gagement—had 19,000 troops to get the job done. He divided them between Manhattan and Brooklyn and set them to building fortifications, with special emphasis on protecting the Brooklyn Heights, for the British were expected to land on Long Island and press through Brooklyn toward Manhattan.

On the night of Aug. 26, 1776, thousands of Britain's troops began landing on the south shore of Long Island, southeast of Brooklyn Heights. Then General Howe executed a brilliant maneuver: although his men had landed on the right flank of the colonial lines, 10,000 of them quickly marched nine miles north across the island. By 9 a.m. on Aug. 27 this column arrived, completely undetected, at the left flank of the American lines—the last place from which the colonials expected an attack.

At 9 a.m. signal cannons sounded, and 22,000 imperial troops, including 7,000 kilted Highland warriors from Scotland and 5,000 Hessian mercenaries, launched a three-pronged attack on the 3,100 Americans below the Heights. Outnumbered and outgeneraled, the colonials crumbled before the assault, fleeing to the fortifications above them with grievous losses.

A badly beaten Washington initially resolved to defend the Heights but soon realized the British were too powerful. On the night of Aug. 29-30, 9,000 colonials slipped away, crossing the East River on small boats in a brilliant mini-Dunkirk that saved the army to fight another day. The British gave chase, if tardily, landing at Kip's Bay on the east shore of Manhattan on Sept. 15. Here Washington rode into the heat of the battle, using his whip on his fleeing soldiers in an attempt to rally them. He was unsuccessful, and the retreat continued, although the troops abused by Washington won back some of their confidence by helping other colonials put up a strong stand at the Harlem Heights the next day, repelling a British attack.

It was a narrow escape: a more energetic British general might have annihilated Washington's army. But safe evacuations and rearguard actions do not win wars. The British marched on, quickly capturing two key fortresses along the Hudson, Fort Washington and Fort Lee. By late fall, George Washington's army was alive and functioning—barely. In three months he had lost New York City, lost his reputation with the Congress and lost the confidence of some of his chief lieutenants. Washington, the army and the Revolution were on the ropes. ∎

New Jersey's General William Alexander, holding the right flank of the colonial lines, leads his men against overwhelming odds

George Washington, in defeat at Kip's Bay

The Christmas Crossing

Eluding pursuit, moving quickly and striking swiftly, Washington finds success after months of failures at the **battles of Trenton and Princeton**

GEORGE WASHINGTON WAS ON THE RUN. THE DATE WAS Dec. 1, 1776, and the Continental Army was reeling in retreat from the British and their Hessian mercenaries. Bragging to his cohorts that he was going to snag Washington as a hunter bags a fox, Lord Cornwallis and his troops were hot on the trail of the 3,400 colonials quick-marching from Newark, N.J., toward New Brunswick. The race was so close that Washington's troops could only partially disable the bridge over which they crossed the Raritan River before a Hessian advance guard showed up.

The Americans eluded the British, then retreated further, crossing the Delaware River into Pennsylvania at Trenton by boat and burning any other boats for miles around. By now, the colonials had mastered the art of the retreat; success in the advance was yet to be acquired. In the past few months, the rebels had fallen back from Brooklyn to Manhattan, from Manhattan north to White Plains, from White Plains west to New Jersey. Along the way, the British had taken control of New York City and two valuable fortresses on the Hudson River, Fort Lee and Fort

Washington, and General Washington had committed a number of strategic blunders that left Congress and his lieutenants questioning his abilities. Earlier, when Washington had urged General Charles Lee to move the 7,000 troops still at White Plains to join his force in New Jersey, Lee had taken his time: failure by Washington might give the ambitious Lee his job. Lee and his army finally showed up in New Jersey in early December, but he was captured by the British in the act of writing a letter to his colleague, General Horatio Gates, that criticized Washington. From history's point of view, the British bagged the right fox.

With winter approaching and rebel spirits everywhere in decline, Washington knew he must strike back;. Many of his troops' enlistments would expire on Jan. 1, and when the Delaware River froze, he might again be on the run. The general conceived a bold plan: to strike by surprise under the cover of darkness, crossing the Delaware himself at a time when the nearest adversaries, the 1,200 Hessians under Colonel Johann Rall at Trenton, would least expect it: Christmas night.

Emanuel Leutze's famous 1851 image of the crossing is not accurate, but it conveys a sense of the magnitude of the undertaking

"I crossed over to Jersey ... about 9 miles above Trenton with upwards of

Three rebel forces assembled. The main body of 2,400 men and 18 cannons under Washington would cross nine miles above Trenton, two smaller units under General James Ewing and Colonel John Cadwallader at Trenton Ferry and Bordentown. In the event, only Washington's group was able to make the passage, for the Delaware on Christmas night was swirling with jagged floes of ices, tossed about in a raging current. The weather delayed the crossing; it wasn't until 4 a.m. that the men had assembled on the New Jersey side and began marching, with their hopes of striking before dawn lost.

Washington still held his strongest card: the element of sur-

prise. As his troops approached the Hessian barracks from five directions, silence hung over them. Hung over as well were the camp's commander and his men; they had mounted such an effective campaign on the wassail bowl on Christmas night that Colonel Rall had to be carried to his bed.

The battle that followed roared through the streets of Trenton, but the colonials never lost the offensive. Muskets were useless in the bad weather, and the Americans overwhelmed the Hessians with bayonets and cannon fire. By 9:30, 106 Germans were dead and 918 captured—and Washington had utterly reversed the flow of the war. Elated with their victory, most of his troops signed up for six more weeks of fighting, and Washington soon put them to work. After a few days of rest, he crossed back into New Jersey, taking up a position outside Trenton, where Cornwallis was heading with his troops. On the night of Jan. 2, Washington again outfoxed the British; leaving a token force behind to represent his full army, he led a stealthy evacuation toward Princeton and New Brunswick. His men surprised 1,200 British under Lieut. Colonel Charles Mawhood at Princeton the next morning; at first the Americans buckled under a barrage of musket fire, but Washington personally rallied them, and the British fled.

Washington's men were exhausted and could not push on to New Brunswick, denying the general a great prize: a huge cache of supplies and a war chest of some £70,000 the British had stashed there. But Washington's two brisk victories had purchased something money couldn't buy: he had regained the trust of Congress and his generals, and he had proved that the colonials were in the war to stay. ∎

MANSELL COLLECTION—TIME LIFE PICTURES

2000 Men and attacked three Regiments of Hessians" —Washington

Chronicles of War: 1777

Sprawling across half a continent and lasting six years, the Revolutionary War was fought on four major fronts: upstate New York and New England; New Jersey, Pennsylvania and downstate New York; the South, including the coastal cities of Savannah and Charleston and the interior of North Carolina; and along the Western frontier, where the British and their Native American allies kept up a steady war of terror against settlers. Yet it was a fifth front—the diplomatic front in France, where U.S. representatives Ben Franklin Silas Deane, John Adams and others lobbied for French aid—that perhaps played the most critical role in the colonies' eventual triumph. France, still smarting from its defeat by the British in the Seven Years War, which ended its empire in North America, was always eager to counter the interests of its longtime rival.

The Continental Congress and George Washington were acutely aware that they must convince the French that they had a chance of winning the war before the French would lend serious support to the colonial cause. That turning point came after the British army under

General John Burgoyne surrendered at Saratoga, N.Y., in October 1777. Within months, France agreed to recognize the United States and entered into a formal alliance with the colonies. Thanks to this diplomatic victory, badly needed supplies and war matériel began flowing to the U.S. (In fact, France had been channeling supplies in secret to the rebels since the war began.) Direct French military support was not so helpful at first: a large French fleet under Admiral Charles Hector d'Estaing sailed to the colonies in the summer of 1778 but proved ineffective, and a combined Franco-American attack on British-held Savannah in October 1779 was a fiasco.

In 1780 the British shifted the focus of the war to the South, scoring early success, but the rebels fought back under new commander Nathaniel Greene, beating the British in 1781 at the Battle of Cowpens and holding them to a tie at Guilford Courthouse. In 1782 the Franco-American alliance proved victorious when a French ground army and fleet teamed up with Washington to bottle up General Charles Cornwallis and his troops at Yorktown, Va., ending the war. ■

With Washington in the background, General Mercer is killed, bottom center, at Brandywine

Brandywine: 1777

On Aug. 24, 1777, General George Washington paraded his Continental Army, some 11,000 men strong, through the streets of Philadelphia, the largest city in America and, as the home of the Second Continental Congress, the capital of the Revolution. This show of force was intended to impress the citizens of the city, where many Loyalists sided with the British, as well as the commander of British forces in America, General William Howe, who had decided to attempt a knockout blow on the rebels by capturing Philadelphia for the Crown. The cautious Howe was taking the long way to Philadelphia from New York City, which the British had occupied since Washington's retreat after the battles of Long Island and Kip's Bay the previous summer.

Howe's troops landed some 60 miles south of Philadelphia, in Maryland, the day after Washington's parade. The two armies finally bumped up against each other near Brandywine Creek, Pa., on Sept. 10. Here, once again, Howe, General Charles Cornwallis and the new Hessian commander Baron Wilhelm von Knyphausen, completely outgeneraled the Americans. As at the Battle of Long Island, Howe dispatched a small diversionary force against the American positions east of Brandywine Creek from the west while quickly marching the bulk of his men in a roundabout flanking move to the north, allowing them to attack the unsuspecting northern flank of the Continental forces and overwhelm them. When the Hessians broke the Continentals' center, the battle turned into a rout. Washington and his generals retreated toward Philadelphia, fighting a series of delaying actions that were unable to stop the British advance.

In late September, the British marched unopposed into Philadelphia; Congress had fled. Determined that his army still seem viable, Washington attacked the bulk of Howe's troops on Oct. 4 at Germantown, Pa.; again, he was defeated, although his gutsy attack won the respect of his men—and of the French. Washington now withdrew to set up winter quarters at Valley Forge.

Princeton: 1777

Following his brilliant surprise attack at Trenton, Washington settled his army into a camp along the nearby Assumpink Creek. British troops under General Charles Cornwallis were gathering around the Continental Army's position on the night of Jan. 2, planning to attack the next day. That night, showing his expertise at stealth operations, Washington left some 400 men in the camp, tending enough bonfires to suggest that the full army was still in residence; in fact, the bulk of the Continentals began marching quietly out of the camp at 1 a.m. on Jan. 3. The troops reached Princeton by morning, just in time to engage two British units, led by Lieut. Colonel Charles Mawhood, that were marching toward Trenton.

In a brief battle that followed, the Americans under General Hugh Mercer tangled with the British in an orchard field; when it looked as if the Continental line might not hold, Washington rode into the thick of the battle, rallying the troops. Mercer was killed, but the Americans held the field; the British retreated, and Washington had won the second of two critical victories. A third, however, eluded him: the road was open to Brunswick, site of a British supply depot, where he might have seized badly needed supplies and a huge war chest. But his troops were too exhausted to carry on; the army went, very late, into winter quarters at Morristown, N.J., having restored some of the pride it had lost in its retreat from New York City.

A local farmer, Squire Cheney, informs Washington that he is about to be surrounded at Brandywine

Victory's Cold Crucible

Cannons standing sentinel over a winter scene at modern-day Valley Forge evoke the 18th century, when war was a warm-weather sport—technology had yet to make combat in the cold a practical option for large armies. In December 1777 the English set up winter quarters in the comfort of Philadelphia, which they had captured three months before, and whiled away the season at concerts, dances and sumptuous feasts. (Ben Franklin noted that General William Howe had not taken Philadelphia so much as Philadelphia had taken him.) George Washington, by contrast, chose as his winter redoubt a field alongside the Schuylkill River about 25 miles from Philadelphia—Valley Forge.

The 10,000 troops that stumbled into Valley Forge six days before Christmas were in desperate condition. Their general later remembered, without exaggeration, that their path could be traced in snow turned crimson by their blood. Before the coming of spring, 1 in 4 of them would starve, freeze to death or succumb to disease; thousands more deserted. Yet most stayed at their posts. For those who remained, Valley Forge would mark a turning point, after which they and the war they were fighting would never be the same.

While the British grew fat and weak in Philadelphia, Washington's band of untrained, ill-equipped irregulars became a genuine army of professional soldiers. The general drilled and schooled them relentlessly, assisted by Baron Friedrich von Steuben, a brilliant Prussian officer who had rallied to the American cause, while a new quartermaster, Nathanael Greene, worked to resolve the supply problems that had plagued the Continental Army from its earliest days.

The men Washington led back onto the field of combat in June 1778 were better trained, better equipped and better led than ever before. And now a fresh breeze was blowing at their back: the month before, France had declared war on England and pledged to fight alongside Washington's troops. ∎

Valley Forge

... Nothing but virtue has kept our army together." —Colonel John Brooks

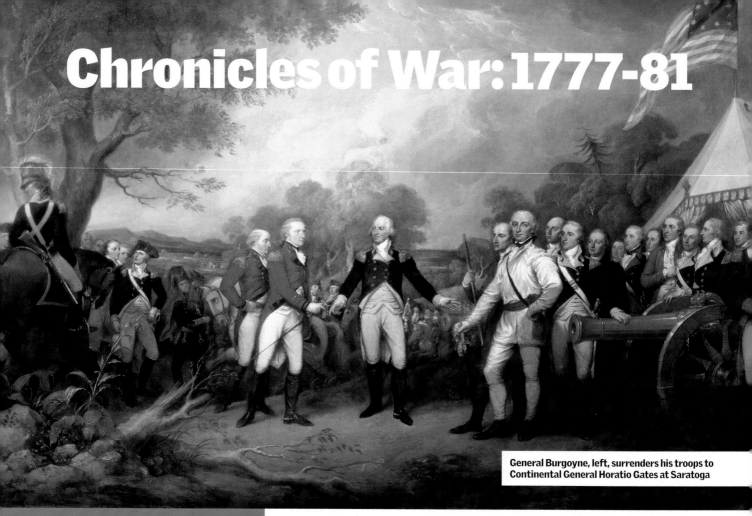

Chronicles of War: 1777-81

General Burgoyne, left, surrenders his troops to Continental General Horatio Gates at Saratoga

Saratoga: 1777

One British scheme for ending the Revolution quickly involved cutting off rebellious New England by taking control of the Hudson River, isolating the region, then squeezing it into submission. The charge fell to the dashing General John Burgoyne, who planned to land an expedition force from Newfoundland at Lake Champlain and move south along the Hudson, meeting up with Britain's top commander, General William Howe, at Albany. Howe had other ideas: he moved south to occupy Philadelphia.

Yet Burgoyne proceeded, landing 7,000 troops in late June 17, 1777, and marching to Fort Ticonderoga, which he succeeded in capturing in early July. But he suffered severe losses at the Battle of Bennington, then was thoroughly whipped in a two-stage battle at Saratoga, at Freeman's Farm and Bemis Heights.

In both actions, it was the American General Benedict Arnold who rallied the troops, even as the real commander, General Horatio Gates, dithered. When Burgoyne's surrounded troops surrendered on Oct. 17, it was a turning point for the rebels' cause.

In frigid winter weather, George Rogers Clark , right, marched his men 150 miles in 18 days to take the British fort at Vincennes in today's Indiana

Vincennes: 1779

In the Western territories, far from Philadelphia, Saratoga and Valley Forge, the British and their Indian allies waged a grisly, ongoing war of terror against the settlers in which torture, mutilation, scalping and even ritual cannibalism were employed. After the Native Americans, led by Mohawk Chief Joseph Brant, won a series of victories in Pennsylvania in 1778, Washington sent General John Sullivan and 2,400 men into the region; they succeeded in putting Brant on the defensive. Further west, in the territories that would become Ohio, Illinois and Indiana, George Rogers Clark led a Virginia militia unit on a spectacular campaign, taking control of British forts at Kaskasia and Cahokia (Illinois) in 1778 and Vincennes (Indiana) in 1779. But Rogers failed to win his ultimate goal, Fort Detroit in today's Michigan.

Cowpens: 1781

The British had attempted to take over the key port city of Charleston, S.C., in June 1776, but had been repulsed. Two years later they returned to the South, easily capturing Savannah, Ga., on Dec. 29, 1778. They would hold the city until July 1782, fighting off a combined U.S.-French effort to retake it in October 1779. The British finally managed to take Charleston in May 1780, after a large force under General Henry Clinton laid siege to the rebels inside; when 5,000 Americans surrendered, it was the biggest patriot defeat of the war.

The British scored again at Camden, S.C., where they mauled the rebels in August 1780. But the pendulum swung with two rebel victories, at King's Mountain, N.C., on Oct. 7, 1780, and at Cowpens, S.C., on Jan. 17, 1781. These battles kept North Carolina free of British influence and put a halt to Britain's string of successes in the South.

The Americans under General Dan Morgan routed British General Banestre Tarleton at Cowpens

The British won the day at Guilford Courthouse, but at a deadly cost, and the war dragged on

Guilford Courthouse: 1781

The string of British victories in the South was largely the result of poor American leadership. Finally, after three generals chosen by Congress had failed, George Washington was allowed to choose the top commander for the region; he named Nathaniel Greene, a highly capable man who had been at his side in critical battles. Greene split his forces, sending the brilliant General Dan Morgan to beat the British at Cowpens. Meanwhile, Greene's troops were pursued by General Charles Cornwallis north to the Dan River near Virginia. Fi-nally, Greene took a stand at Guilford Courthouse, N.C., on March 15, 1781. Here the British scored a technical victory, holding their place on the field. But Cornwallis lost at least a quarter of his army in the battle and had to withdraw from North Carolina's interior. The battles at Cowpens and Guilford Courthouse further convinced Parliament and the British public that there would be no easy victory in the war, thus setting the stage for its long-awaited conclusion, with the surrender of Cornwallis' army at Yorktown, Va., six months later.

Endgame at Yorktown

Trapped between the French navy and the combined armies of the
colonies and France, General Cornwallis agrees to a **British surrender**

American General Benjamin Lincoln, center, leads
surrendering British troops in this John Trumbull
painting; Washington is mounted behind on a
dark horse. Cornwallis pleaded illness and did not
attend the surrender ceremony

FOR YEARS, THE CENTRAL STRATEGIC FACT OF THE REVO-
lutionary War was Britain's control of America's coastal
waters. When George Washington wanted to move his
troops, they had to walk, whereas the British army could quickly and easily sail anywhere from Boston to Savannah. Even after France sent an army of 6,000 men, under the command of
General Jean-Baptiste Rochambeau, to help the Continental
cause in 1780, it mattered little. Without a fleet, the troops were
stranded in Newport, R.I., for almost a year, during which time
the focus of the war shifted far away, to the South.

But in the spring of 1781, the Marquis de Lafayette, America's greatest champion in Paris, persuaded King Louis XVI to
send a fleet, under the brilliant admiral François de Grasse,
to tip the scales against the British. Carrying 4,000 fresh
troops, De Grasse arrived on Aug. 5 at Chesapeake Bay, where
he surprised and mauled the Royal Navy's fleet. This flawlessly
executed ambush climaxed just as Britain's General Charles
Cornwallis was marching his troops through Virginia toward
the coast, where he planned to link up with British vessels at
Yorktown. When he found these waters in the hands of the
French fleet, Cornwallis knew he was in trouble.

Just how much trouble would become clear in the next few
weeks. While De Grasse was boxing Cornwallis in from the
Atlantic, Washington and Rochambeau were marching at top
speed toward Virginia from the north. When their troops took
up positions on the inland side of Cornwallis' encampment
and de Grasse began landing his troops from the coastal side,
the British general found himself completely surrounded.
The combined American and French forces totalled more
than 16,000 men, while Cornwallis had less than half that
number under his command. Still, the British general held out
for almost 10 weeks, hoping to be relieved by the British garrison in New York, commanded by General Henry Clinton.
But as Washington's and Rochambeau's troops began a
bloody siege of the British positions, and it became clear that
no help was on the way, Cornwallis bowed to the inevitable.

When he signed the surrender documents on Oct. 19, 1781,
Cornwallis effectively ended Britain's hopes for victory over
the rebellious colonies. As sullen British soldiers marched
through the Continental lines to give up their weapons, colonial military bands played a popular air, *The World Turned Up-
side Down.* In London, King George III went so far as to draft
a letter of abdication, though he never submitted it to Parliament. One letter that was dispatched, however, was Cornwallis' final message to his commander, General Clinton, in
New York. "I have the mortification to inform your excellen-
cy," he began, "that I have been forced to give up the posts ...
and to surrender the troops under my command, by capitula-
tion, on the 19th instant ... to the combined forces of America and France." After six years, the war was over ∎

Freedom: Made in France

After long years of war, exhausted Britons realize they can no longer fight inspired rebels a long ocean away, and they sign the 1783 **Treaty of Paris**

I N THE WAKE OF THE AMERICANS' GREAT VICTORY AT YORK-town in 1781, the major question facing both the former colonists and the British was, "What's next?" Clearly, the six-year war was nearly over: the rebellious colonies had won. But exactly when and how hostilities would actually end—and the determination of precisely what it was, exactly, that the Americans had won—were still far from obvious.

George Washington would later call the 23 months of suspense after Yorktown the most dangerous period of the war. His French allies had gone home. His own army was disintegrating from exhaustion. But the English still controlled every important seaport between New York and Savannah, as well as major cities like Detroit, and they remained masters of the ocean all along the Atlantic Coast. Fighting with Native American tribes sponsored by the British continued on the Western frontiers. If they had chosen that moment to strike, the English might still have won. Indeed, if the British mere-

ly insisted on keeping the territory they held at the end of the war, the young nation would have been landlocked. "We are enveloped in darkness," Washington wrote at the time.

Fiat lux! The British had lost the will to continue fighting. In February 1782, the government resigned; it was succeeded by a pro-American faction that quickly opened peace negotiations in Paris, mediated by the French. The Treaty of Paris was signed on Sept. 3, 1783, and was a diplomatic triumph for U.S. envoys John Jay, Ben Franklin, Henry Laurens and John Adams. Britain recognized independence and ceded all the territory between the Atlantic and the Mississippi, south of Canada and north of the Gulf of Mexico (excepting New Orleans and Spain's colony in Florida), to the new United States of America. King George III, his royal pride wounded, consoled himself with the thought that America would have been a great loss, "did I not also know that knavery seems to be so much the striking feature of its inhabitants." ∎

Benjamin West was unable to complete this portrait of Americans in Paris in 1783. From left, John Jay, John Adams, Benjamin Franklin, South Carolina diplomat Henry Laurens and William Temple Franklin, Ben's son

The Best Brush in Boston

Fine art begins to bloom in the backward colonies; as Revolution looms, **John Singleton Copley** portrays the urban artistocrats of Massachusetts

THE CHILD OF POOR IRISH IMMIGRANTS, JOHN Singleton Copley of Boston had little formal training in art but possessed an innate gift that made him the foremost portrait painter of the young colonies in the 1760s and early '70s, at a time when fine art was beginning to appear in America, previously a cultural backwater. His luminous canvases and exquisite brushwork reveal Boston's gentry as they wanted to be seen: prosperous, accomplished, reserved. In addition to the works shown here, Copley painted the portraits of Paul Revere and Samuel Adams earlier in the book; the inset above is a self-portrait painted when Copley was in his early 40s.

Copley was first and forever an artist, not a patriot: in 1774, when the growing turmoil that would lead to the Revolution began to make commissions hard to come by, he left Boston for Britain, where he enjoyed great success. Before his death in 1815, he branched out to produce large-scale outdoor scenes. His fine delineations of America's wealthiest citizens show us a world that would be put on hold during the turbulence of the Revolution, when the subjects he portrayed faced the most difficult of choices: to throw in with the rebels or support the Crown. ∎

Mr. and Mrs. Thomas Miflin, 1773

Mrs. Joseph Scott, c. 1765

Mrs. James Russell, 1770

Mrs. Thomas Boylston, 1766

Lady in a Blue Dress, 1763

New Yorkers celebrate the adoption of the Constitution, the new "ship of state," and honor local advocate Alexander Hamilton in 1788

Designing a Nation

First Steps: 1781-1804

1781
Articles of Confederation and Perpetual Union approved by Congress

1783
The Treaty of Paris ends the war and recognizes the U.S. as a nation

1787
Constitutional Convention drafts new Constitution in Philadelphia

1788
The Constitution is ratified

1789
George Washington is inaugurated as President in New York City, temporary capital of U.S.

1790
New Federal District planned for area carved out of Virginia and Maryland; Philadelphia is temporary capital

1791
Bill of Rights enumerating personal freedoms is added to the Constitution

1792
Washington re-elected President

1795
Jay Treaty avoids war with Britain but is highly unpopular with Americans.

1797
John Adams becomes second President

1798
Congress passes Alien and Sedition Acts, widely viewed as unconstitutional

1799
George Washington dies

1800
In unpopular move, Adams avoids war with France over trade disputes; U.S. government moves to new capital city, Washington

1801
Thomas Jefferson becomes third President

1804
Aaron Burr kills Alexander Hamilton in a duel of honor

President George Washington

"I was using my utmost exertions to establish a national character of our own,

Reluctant Executive

GEORGE WASHINGTON NEVER LOOMED LARGER than when he was absent from the scene. His life story has a satisfyingly repetitive quality: Washington distinguishes himself in some great endeavor, then retires, Voltaire-like, to tend his garden at Mount Vernon in Virginia. Suddenly, a messenger arrives: Washington is needed! His country calls! And back into the saddle he clambers, vowing to patient Martha, "I shall return." Thus it was that Washington, who trained to be a surveyor, became a military hero in the French and Indian War, then commander-in-chief of the Continental Army and, finally, first President of the U.S.

Washington's heroic service in the Revolutionary War made him one of the most celebrated people on the planet. Europeans were accustomed to military heroes who grabbed for power; they were shocked when the great general, emulating the Roman warrior Cincinnatus, resigned his commission, refusing to parlay his renown into high office. Even King George III was stunned by the act. "If true," he declared, "then he is the greatest man in the world."

The greatest man in the world enjoyed four years of domestic tranquillity at Mount Vernon after the war, but in 1787, the messenger arrived, and Washington journeyed to Philadelphia, where he presided over the Constitutional Convention. The document called for a single Chief Executive, to be called the "President," and his fellow delegates didn't have to look far to find a candidate. In 1788, the messenger returned: Washington had won all 69 votes in the Electoral College.

The old soldier, now 57, had no interest in the office, but he knew well that he was the only person who could summon the states—already deeply divided over issues of size and slavery—into a true union. On April 30, 1789, Washington took the oath of office at Federal Hall in New York City. He helped broker the deal that created a new federal district, fittingly not far from his home on the Potomac River, then laid the cornerstone for the Capitol. He put on his uniform again in 1794, when he led an army to take on the Pennsylvania frontiersmen defying federal tax officials in the Whiskey Rebellion. In his second term he weathered his first taste of unpopularity, when a treaty his envoy John Jay agreed to with Britain was deemed a disgrace by most Americans. Although clearly sympathetic to the Federalists, he feared the factional politics that arose on his watch might sunder the union. He left office in 1797 and died two years later, never looming larger. ∎

This life mask of Washington at age 53 was cast by French sculptor Jean-Antoine Houdon in 1785

Patriot and Partner

WIFE OF THE NATION'S SECOND PRESIDENT and mother of its sixth, Abigail Adams retains a lively grip on the American imagination, thanks to the decades of correspondence she shared with her husband John. Her letters reveal a woman of acute, sardonic intelligence and strong opinions—which, she complained, she found difficult to keep to herself. John Adams referred to her as "my dearest Partner … my best, dearest, worthiest, wisest friend in this World … I think you shine as a Stateswoman."

Abigail Smith was born to politics; her grandfather served more than two decades in the Massachusetts legislature and Supreme Court. Well informed but lacking formal schooling, she was all too aware of women's unequal role in society ("I will never consent to have our sex considered … inferior") and often complained that her education was incomplete. She married John Adams at 20 and they had four children; she steadfastly remained at the family home in Braintree (later Quincy), just south of Boston, while her children's father was off being a Founding Father. Through her frequent letters she kept her husband apprised of local affairs, including the Battle of Bunker Hill, which she watched from a distance. Abigail traveled to France and England in 1784-88 when John was posted there, but the easy morals of the French court and the revealing costumes of Parisian ballerinas were not to her taste.

Though frequently ill when her husband served as the nation's second President, she helped John move into the unfinished White House (which she hated) in 1801, hanging her clothes on a line in the East Room for modesty's sake. When Adams left the presidency shortly after, the two headed for home, where they were finally able to enjoy 17 happy years together, no postage required. ∎

Abigail Adams

"I was always for equality, as my husband can witness."

Hero and Outcast

JOHN JAY WAS AMERICA'S FIRST SECRETARY OF STATE and first Chief Justice, yet for a time he was last in the hearts of his countrymen. A Federalist and close ally of Washington, Adams and Hamilton, his fingerprints are everywhere on the building plans of the new nation, but few other Founding Fathers endured such wide public derision as he. The New York lawyer was president of the Continental Congress in 1778-79, then served as the colonies' envoy to Spain, failing to win its support for the Revolution. With Franklin and Adams, Jay helped negotiate the Treaty of Paris, which ended the war, then became the nation's first Secretary of State under the Articles of Confederation. Aware of the need for a stronger government, he wrote five of the *Federalist* papers, helped shepherd the ratification of the Constitution through the New York Assembly and in 1789 was named the first Chief Justice by President Washington.

Jay was frustrated at the third-rate status of the court; his duties included riding a circuit to hear lower-court lawsuits. He was relieved of this burden in 1794, when Washington asked him to become a special envoy to England. The U.S. and Britain were facing the tensions that would finally erupt in the War of 1812. The English were conspiring with Native Americans to spread terror in the Western territories and were impressing U.S. civilian sailors into their ships at will; the British also refused to reimburse Southern planters for slaves they had liberated during the Revolution. Jay returned with a treaty that most Americans felt was far too weak; it failed to address impressment on the seas or Britain's collaboration with the Indians. Jay was denounced—even Hamilton called him an "old woman"— and hung in effigy in frontier territories. George Washington had to fight hard to get the treaty approved and funded by the House and Senate.

Jay, a tough character, weathered the storm and later served with distinction as Governor of New York, fighting corruption in appointments, reforming the prisons and advancing the bill that gradually abolished slavery in the state. Jay awaits his day; his contributions to American life deserve wider recognition. ∎

John Jay

"The jury has a right to judge both the law as well as the fact in controversy."

Equal to the Occasion

THE BEWIGGED YOUNG DANDY AT LEFT, WHO ARrived at the Second Continental Congress in Philadelphia in 1775 with three liveried servants in tow, looks like the last man on earth who, within the year, would pen one of the most incendiary and liberating phrases in human history: "We hold these truths to be self-evident: that all men are created equal ..." The words made this member of Virginia's slaveholding gentry the worlds' foremost apostle of republican egalitarianism, and that is only the first of the manifold ironies and complexities that make Thomas Jefferson an eternally fascinating character.

Jefferson may have been created equal, but he was born lucky; his father Peter was a successful surveyor who left his son 2,750 acres of prime Virginia land and put him through the College of William and Mary. Bright, lively and ambitious, Thomas studied law and was elected to Virginia's House of Burgesses at only 25. He served in every assembly until he was chosen as a delegate to the Second Congress, following the publication of his powerful 1774 screed against the Crown, *Summary View of the Rights of British America*. In this pamphlet, influenced by British philosopher John Locke and others, he first argued that the rights of man derive from the laws of nature, not the monarchy.

At first Jefferson was one of the more radical voices in the Congress, but the events of 1775 and the first months of '76 proved his prescience, and when the time came to draft a Declaration of Independence, the fiery young redhead—who was an awkward public speaker but a brilliant writer—was a natural choice for the task. No one could imagine that Jefferson would write a document whose soaring words would continue to inspire and challenge mankind centuries after they were written, but as Thomas Paine noted, these were the times that tried men's souls, and when Jefferson's soul was tried, he proved equal to the challenge. ∎

Thomas Jefferson

"I hold it, that a little rebellion, now and then, is a good thing, and as necessary in the political word as storms in the physical."

Some Kind of Genius

ALEXANDER HAMILTON'S LIFE WAS BOOKENDED by scandal: he was born a bastard and died in a duel. Yet he was one of the great shapers of the nation, always at George Washington's side, it seemed, whether the setting was a battlefield in New Jersey rallying the troops; Independence Hall in Philadelphia as the Constitution was being hammered out; or an office in New York City, serving as America's first Secretary of the Treasury. On this page, as in life, he faces the man who became his most ardent foe, Thomas Jefferson; each of them was a magnetic figure who attracted others to his cause. The twin poles of the early Republic, they founded the party system in American politics.

Hamilton was born on the Caribbean island of Nevis in 1755. His early life resembles a Dickens novel: his mother died at 11, his father went bankrupt, and young Hamilton became a clerk in a counting house. Yet his intellect and willpower carried him to America, to a degree from King's College (now Columbia University) and to a 1778 appointment as Washington's personal aide. He excelled in every endeavor he undertook: as a soldier, he rallied the troops at Monmouth and Yorktown. As a political theorist, his probing essays in the *Federalist* papers argued for a strong Federal Government to hold the states together. As the moneyman of the early Republic, he founded, against great opposition, the national bank that helped put the young nation on a sound fiscal footing.

His politics bears the stamp of one whose good fortune is the residue of his own design: Hamilton was a cynical, wised-up realist who believed that lofty blather couldn't sustain a nation, but a fiscally sound dollar could; and that self-interest, not love of others, was the prime mover in most men's lives. That he was a genius no one could deny. Jefferson preferred to add a critical adjective to that noun: he called his adversary "the evil genius of America." ∎

Alexander Hamilton

"A fondness for power is implanted, in most men, and it is natural to abuse it"

Supreme Being

IMAGINE AN AMERICA IN WHICH CONGRESSMEN assail federal judges and demand their impeachment, while Presidents scheme to place friendly judges into office in their last moments of power. If conjuring such a vision isn't much of a stretch, it's because the issues that John Marshall faced more than 200 years ago are fundamental to the checks and balances built into the Constitution. The nation's fourth Chief Justice and the most influential jurist in its history, the gifted Virginian was an officer in the Revolutionary War, wrote a five-volume biography of George Washington, served a term in Congress and was John Adams' Secretary of State. A clubbable man, Marshall loved Jane Austen and the theater—as well as barbecue, a glass of punch and a friendly game of quoits, a precursor of horseshoes.

When Adams named Marshall Chief Justice in 1800, the judiciary was by far the weakest of the three branches of the Federal Government. Tellingly, Pierre L'Enfant hadn't even given the court a home in his plan for Washington, D.C., and the Justices first met in a cramped basement room in the Capitol. But when new President Thomas Jefferson tried to countermand Adams' naming of Federalist-leaning judges in the last hours of his presidency by refusing to deliver their commissions, Marshall's court ruled that the congressional act Jefferson was using to justify his course was unconstitutional. This decision in the case of *Marbury v. Madison* (1803) firmly established the principle of judicial review of Congress while confirming the Court's independence from the Executive Branch. Serving more than 34 years as Chief Justice, Marshall also established the precedence of the federal courts over state courts and freed interstate commerce from restrictive state legislation. Defying L'Enfant, Marshall put the Court where it remains—at the center of American life. ∎

John Marshall

"The acme of judicial distinction means the ability to look a lawyer straight in the eyes for two hours and not hear a damned word he says."

Benjamin Banneker

"We are a race of beings, who have long labored under the abuse and censure of the world."

BANNAKER.

A Man in Full

NO ONE DOUBTS THAT BENJAMIN BANNEKER WAS A REMARK-able man, but there is some debate over the exact extent of his achievements. The grandson of a freed slave named Bannaky, Benjamin was a farmer, mathematical wizard and a self-taught surveyor. He showed mathematical promise from an early age, despite an impoverished upbringing and a rudimentary education. At age 21, he was given a Swiss pocket watch, which so fascinated him that he took it apart, drew its parts, then re-created them from wood; the resulting clock struck on the hour until his death. A student of the stars, he correctly predicted a solar eclipse in 1789 and published an almanac for the Pennsylvania, Delaware, Maryland and Vir-

ginia region for 11 years, from 1791 to 1802 (the 1795 title page is above, with an alternate spelling of his name).

Banneker's expertise as a surveyor was known to George Washington, who hired him to help survey the nation's new Federal District in 1791. Some accounts say that after Pierre L'Enfant was dismissed as architect of the capital and took his plans with him, Banneker re-created them from memory; that story is questionable. In 1792 Banneker wrote a long letter to Thomas Jefferson disputing his conclusion in *Notes on the State of Virginia* (1787), that blacks were intellectually inferior; Jefferson wrote an ambiguous reply. But it was Banneker's life, not his letter, that put the lie to Jefferson's argument. ■

Some Assembly Required

When the Articles of Confederation prove too weak to forge a strong Union, brilliant collaborators create a powerful new **U.S. Constitution**

WHEN, IN THE COURSE OF HUMAN EVENTS, SENSIBLE people make bad choices, they take a deep breath and start over again. Such was the case with the men who had won the American Revolution in the years after their triumph. The Founding Fathers had achieved independence. Yet their new nation just wasn't working.

The problem was black and white—literally. The jurisdiction and powers of the U.S. federal government, as spelled out in the Articles of Confederation and Perpetual Union, adopted by Congress in 1781, were too weak. The Confederation Congress looked and sounded like a government, but it was actually little more than a forum of regional politicians with few interests in common who viewed one another with suspicion—and had no power to levy taxes, raise armies or even enact (much less

enforce) its own laws. In short, it was today's United Nations in powdered wigs and hosiery.

The problems were obvious, and attempts were made to revise the Articles from the moment they were adopted. But many individual states were reluctant to cede any of their newfound sovereignty to a stronger central government: that smacked of the tyranny they had just thrown off. Even worse, the Articles required unanimous agreement among all 13 states for any changes—a prescription for paralysis.

By 1786, the Articles' drawbacks (especially their failure to regulate chaotic interstate commerce) led the Virginia legislature to invite all the states to send delegates to a convention in Annapolis, Md., "to take into consideration the trade of the United States." Representatives of only five states showed up,

In this fanciful painting, George Washington presides over the delegates Thomas Jefferson described as "an assembly of demi-gods." Neither Jefferson nor John Adams took part in the proceedings, as both were serving as U.S. ambassadors in Europe at the time

were, in the fine phrase of historian James MacGregor Burns, the nation's "well-bred, well-fed, well-wed, and well-read." A consensus quickly emerged that the new Constitution would divide the Federal Government into three branches: the Legislative Branch would be joined by Executive and Judicial bodies, neither of which existed under the Articles. Each branch would be assigned clear responsibilities, and, significantly, each would act as a check on the others' powers.

Debate centered on the structure of the new Congress, where the interests of large and small, free and slave states, must be balanced. James Madison championed the Virginia Plan, which proposed two houses, both of which assigned more members (and more votes) to the larger states. William Patterson countered with the New Jersey Plan, which called for a single house and equal representation for all the states. By July, members of the Connecticut delegation had brokered the Great Compromise, providing for a House of Representatives, which assigned seats in proportion to a state's population, and a Senate, in which every state, no matter its size, would have an equal number of votes.

Other compromises followed. The nation's powerful Chief Executive would be elected, rather than appointed by the Senate—but not directly by the people. Instead, an Electoral College would cast votes on the people's behalf. The Southern states insisted that their slave populations be counted when assigning seats in the House of Representatives, even though no one seriously considered giving the right to vote to anyone other than white men. This resulted in the "Three-Fifths Compromise," in which 60% of a state's slave population would be added to its free population when assigning seats in the House. Sadly, the new nation's founding document sanctioned slavery: at the insistence of Southern states, the Constitution specifically prohibited Congress from passing any laws that abolished or restricted the slave trade until 1808.

Finally, on Sept. 17, 1787, the delegates concluded debate and submitted their work to the Confederation Congress. Containing seven Articles and running to about 4,000 words, the Constitution was an instruction manual for creating a new government. Its most glaring omission (and one that nearly scuttled it) was the lack of a Bill of Rights to guarantee individual freedoms to citizens. Several states ratified the Constitution only on the condition that the new Congress immediately amend it with a clear statement of personal freedoms.

The ratification process, which required each state to hold its own convention to accept or reject the Constitution, began that same month and lasted until June 1788, when New Hampshire became the required ninth state to ratify. Adoption was immeasurably aided by the work of Hamilton, John Jay and Madison: under the shared pseudonym Publius, they wrote 85 newspaper essays, the *Federalist* papers, in which they argued eloquently for ratification and explored, brilliantly, the purpose and structures of democratic government.

All this was still in the future when Benjamin Franklin emerged from the State House in Philadelphia at the end of the Constitutional Convention. Mystified by the assembly's secrecy, a woman approached him and asked, "Well Doctor, what have we got, a republic or a monarchy?" To which Franklin replied, "A republic—if you can keep it." ∎

but they were persuaded by two of the leading advocates for reforming the Articles, Alexander Hamilton and James Madison, to propose a convention to draft a new Constitution.

Every state except Rhode Island sent delegates to Philadelphia in May 1787. Their mission was strictly limited to revising the Articles of Confederation, but some delegates had other ideas. George Washington, who was quickly elected president of the convention, believed the U.S. would not survive unless the central government were strengthened. Ben Franklin agreed. James Madison and Alexander Hamilton went further: Hamilton believed that the U.S. government should be modeled on Britain's, while Madison wanted a legal code that would enshrine property rights above all else.

The 55 delegates who assembled at Independence Hall

Freedom, by the Numbers

The Constitution created a strong central government but overlooked essential personal freedoms, until the states approved the **Bill of Rights**

"I T HAS NO DECLARATION OF RIGHTS," VIRGINIA STATESMAN George Mason complained bitterly when the text of the new U.S. Constitution—which he had helped write—became public in September 1787. Although 55 delegates had attended the Constitutional Convention in Philadelphia, only 39 of them put their signatures to the finished document. Mason was among those who withheld his imprimatur to protest the missing enumeration of personal liberties that, many felt, was an indispensible counterweight to the vast expansion of government power outlined in the document.

Thus began a long, bitter fight: from the moment the Constitution was finished, many Americans wanted to finish it off. "What can avail your specious, imaginary balances, your rope-dancing, chain-rattling, ridiculous … checks and contrivances?" thundered Patrick Henry, who had refused even to attend the convention, so offensive did he find the idea of a strong central government. The opposition to the Constitution began with those who were passionate about the need for a listing of specific rights and guarantees for individuals but grew to include those (like Henry) who were more generally opposed to any broadening of government authority.

The men who had drafted the Constitution decided against including a Bill of Rights in the original version on insufficient grounds: the issue arose late in their deliberations, when most of the delegates were exhausted and wanted to adjourn. What's more, several protections for individual liberty (such as a ban on suspending writs of habeas corpus and a prohibition against retroactive laws) were specified in the document. Those that were not mentioned, went the reasoning of the Federalists (as the advocates for ratification began calling themselves), were clearly implied. Additionally, each of the 13 state constitutions contained a Bill of Rights, and many of the framers believed that this made a similar listing in the federal Constitution unnecessary.

The Federalists soon recognized their mistake. In the battle for public opinion, the anti-Federalists won early victories by underscoring the potential for tyranny contained in this blueprint for a central government far stronger than most Americans had ever envisioned. The Constitution, they argued, should enumerate not only the operation of the nation's government but also the personal rights of its citizens. The document was finally approved in its original form after two years of debate—but just barely, and only on the condition (demanded by ratifying conventions in several states) that

"A bill of rights is what the people are entitled to against every government

Those who took part in the great civil-rights march of 1963 in Washington were asserting their First Amendment rights to assemble peacefully, speak freely and criticize their government without fear

Congress quickly take up consideration of a Bill of Rights.

In his first Inaugural Address, President George Washington urged Congress to begin amending the Constitution, guided by "a reverence for the characteristic rights of freemen, and a regard for the public harmony." Virginian James Madison, the "Father of the Constitution," took the lead in drafting the list of personal freedoms, basing his work largely on the 1776 Virginia Declaration of Rights written by George Mason. (Mason, for his part, had borrowed heavily from England's 1689 Bill of Rights.) Madison's final draft included 13 proposed changes to the Constitution.

The Senate dropped one of Madison's amendments, which forbade the states from abridging the rights of individuals protected by the Constitution. (A similar measure would be enacted as the 14th Amendment in 1868.) Two others, relating to how many constituents each Congressman should represent and the timing of congressional pay raises, were included in the measures sent to the states for approval but were mostly ignored, as irrelevant to personal rights.

The remaining 10 amendments, which enumerated the personal freedoms upon which any democracy must be founded—ranging from freedom of speech and religion to the rights of the accused in criminal proceedings—formed the heart of the package of amendments that were referred to the states for ratification in September 1789. Two months later, New Jersey became the first of the 11 states needed to approve them. More than two years passed before Virginia became the last state to ratify, and the Bill of Rights, the engine of American freedom, acquired the force of law on Dec. 15, 1791. ■

The Bill of Rights, in Brief

Like the Declaration of Independence and the main text of the Constitution, the Bill of Rights has not only served Americans well but has also been employed as a guide for democracies around the world in defining the relationships between citizens, their government and the rule of law. Many of the hot-button issues that divide Americans in the 21st century—from freedom of speech to prayer in the schools to gun control—are addressed in this document, which is now more than two centuries old.

First Amendment In unmistakably clear language ("Congress shall make no law ... "), this powerful amendment guarantees six basic liberties for Americans: freedom of speech and the press; freedom of religion and the separation of church and state; the right to assemble peacefully and the right to petition the government to address grievances.

Second Amendment Provides for the right to bear arms. Legal scholars still debate whether this right was meant to apply only to the now defunct state militias that once made up the bulk of U.S. armed forces or is a general authorization to possess weapons for personal use.

Third Amendment Now dated and irrelevant, this amendment forbids the government to house soldiers in private homes during peacetime without the consent of the owner.

Fourth Amendment Protects against arbitrary searches of "persons, houses, papers, and effects" and bans police from conducting many kinds of search without a court-issued warrant based on "probable cause" that a crime has been committed and that a search will yield significant evidence.

Fifth Amendment Granting all citizens the right to "due process of law," this amendment guarantees that Americans can't be put on trial for a major crime until a grand jury has indicted them; that prosecutors can't try citizens again for the same crime after a prior acquittal; and that the government can't force a citizen to testify against himself.

Sixth Amendment Ensures that those accused of serious crimes have a right to review the charges; to be represented by legal counsel; and to be tried before an impartial jury in a proceeding that is swift, public and near the location of the offense. Also ensures the right to confront and question witnesses.

Seventh Amendment Extends the right of a trial by jury to civil cases in which "the value in controversy shall exceed twenty dollars."

Eighth Amendment Limits the government's ability to punish: bails and fines cannot be excessive, and punishments cannot be "cruel and unusual."

Ninth Amendment Acknowledges that the list of rights contained in the first eight amendments is not all-inclusive and establishes that the people retain other, unspecified rights not mentioned in the Constitution.

Tenth Amendment Reserves every right or power not prohibited by the Constitution—but not specifically granted to the Federal Government—for the individual states and for the people. Many have argued that this amendment seems so broad and self-evident as to be meaningless, including the U.S. Supreme Court, which observed in a 1931 decision that the 10th Amendment "added nothing" to the Constitution.

on earth." —Thomas Jefferson, letter to James Madison, 1787

The Rise of Factions

Stepping off their pedestals, the Founding Fathers who united to create a nation divide over how to govern it, and **political parties** are born

THOMAS JEFFERSON WAS HOLDING FORTH ONE DAY ON the virtues of the common man, explaining that the people are the best and wisest repository of trust and power, when he was interrupted by Alexander Hamilton, who burst out, "Your people, sir, is nothing but a great beast!" This exchange between two men who detested one another reflects the intellectual divisions that began to surface in the years after freedom was won. They are apparent in the text of the Constitution itself, which carefully divides legislative power between lawmakers, who are directly elected by the people and serve terms of only two years; and legislators, who were originally appointed by the most powerful men in their home states (Senators were not elected by popular vote until 1914) to remain in office for six years.

The Founding Fathers had seen Britain's policies toward America shift with every change of power in Parliament; they dreaded sacrificing the national unity they had so desperately forged in the pursuit of political interests. The Constitution they wrote makes no mention of political parties, but as these citizens of the newly united states were soon to find out, parties—or factions, as they were often called at the time—seem essential to the democratic process.

Even before the Revolutionary War was won, American patriots fell into two broad categories: those, like Jefferson, who championed the common man; and those, like Hamilton, who believed in a natural aristocracy and embraced the more gradual march toward limited democracy embodied by English history. Hamilton's camp called the Jeffersonians "levelers," rejecting what they viewed as a radical egalitarianism that would put the dreaded "mob" in power. Jefferson's camp rejoiced in 1789 when France's oppressed multitudes overthrew their King, but when that revolution devolved into an orgy of bloodshed and justice by the guillotine, the Federalists could point to an object lesson in the madness of crowds.

After the war, these long-simmering ideological differences approached the boiling point. As the Articles of Confederation proved unworkable and the need for restructuring the government became apparent, statesmen cleaved into opposing camps, one wishing to strengthen the central government, the other believing that this centralization of power presented a greater danger than the difficulties of governing under the flawed Articles. The first group called themselves Federalists, while the opposition, initially known as Anti-Federalists, eventually became known as the Democratic-Republicans.

Here the lines become blurred. The Constitution's final draft contained many compromises, and the advocates of a more powerful Federal Government failed to achieve many of their goals, including a "president" who was appointed by the Senate to serve for life. For these reasons, some politicians who would later become leaders of the Democratic-Republican Party, including Jefferson and James Madison, supported ratification of the Constitution, albeit reluctantly. Others who would later emerge as leading Federalists, like Hamilton, John Jay and John Adams, also favored ratification but expressed reservations for exactly the reasons that men like Jefferson were willing to endorse the Constitution.

The one man who was consistently able to bridge the divide between these emerging parties was George Washington. Striking a delicate balance and almost always willing to compromise, Washington remained studiously above the fray, describing political parties as "truly the worst enemy" of enlightened government. Even so, America's first President was far more closely identified with Federalist policies than with those of the Democratic-Republicans, and when Washington sided with Hamilton (over Jefferson's objections) to create the first Bank of the United States in hopes of stabilizing the Federal Government's finances, the President came under partisan attack. When he ran for re-election in 1796, Washington did so as a Federalist.

His successor, Adams, embraced policies especially repugnant to Jefferson and the Democratic-Republicans. His misguided attempt to stop the vicious vitriol spewed by his opponents was the Alien and Sedition Acts, which limited their freedom of speech, in clear violation of the First Amendment. In contrast, the Democratic-Republicans were fervent champions of freedom of expression; Jefferson famously claimed he preferred newspapers to governments. The 1800 race between Adams and Jefferson set a high-water mark for invective and slander that has seldom been equalled in American politics.

Jefferson won and scaled back Federalist display when he took office in 1801. His Administration augured the end of the Federalist Party: it would never again hold the presidency and would eventually disappear, discredited in the public eye by its opposition to the War of 1812. But this did not mean the end of partisan rivalry. After a brief period of one-party harmony during the tenure of President James Monroe, the Democratic-Republicans would split into the two perpetually feuding parties that continue to dominate American politics to this day. ■

FIND YOUR FACTION

The first two presidents were Federalists, but the U.S. public gradually moved in the direction of Jefferson's party—although states' rights remained an ever divisive issue

Jefferson

Hamilton

DEMOCRATIC-REPUBLICANS	FEDERALISTS
Leaders: Jefferson, Madison, Monroe	Leaders: Hamilton, Adams, Washington
Focus: common man	Focus: the élite
States' rights	Federal strength
National bank: no	National bank: yes
Agrarian emphasis	Urban emphasis
Favored direct elections and short terms in office	Favored indirect elections and long terms in office
Model: France	Model: Britain

In this Federalist cartoon from 1800, Satan and Jefferson conspire to tear down the nation created by Washington and Adams

A President's Retreat

His admiring contemporaries called John Adams "the Atlas of independence," and indeed the brilliant, irascible Massachusetts lawyer seemed to be lending his support everywhere in the critical years of the early Republic: as a delegate to the First and Second Continental Congresses; as head of the committee that drafted the Declaration of Independence; as a diplomat who helped shape the Treaty of Paris; as the first Vice President and second President. The one place Adams wasn't, however, was where he most longed to be: his farm in a small village south of Boston, Braintree, later known as Quincy.

Adams was born in 1735 in the building at right in the engraving above; his son John Quincy was born in the house at left in 1767, the home of John and Abigail during the years of revolution and war. The main picture shows the kitchen of that small house, where Adams wrote many of the memorable words that carried him to fame. In 1787 Adams purchased a larger nearby home, which he named Peacefield; Abigail expanded that home in 1798, adding a library and study, and it was further enlarged by three more generations of public-spirited Adamses. Today the 11 buildings in this Adams-family compound are preserved as a National Historical Park.

John Adams left Peacefield in 1789 to become the nations' first Vice President, a job he thoroughly hated. His next challenge, the presidency, eluded his grasp. George Washington, who commanded enormous respect from all, had been able to stay aloof from the factional strife now dividing the nation. Adams, unable to summon Washington's lofty remove, found himself attacked, denigrated and whipsawed by the whirlwind of politics. With Philadelphia experiencing annual summertime attacks of yellow fever, the homesick President often retreated to Quincy from the temporary capital. His longest such stay took up the months from March to September 1799; his enemies derided it as an "abdication," and it helped undermine his ability to lead the country. Utterly weary of the presidency, Adams returned home in 1801, to enjoy— at last!—25 years of well-earned rest. ∎

Adams Homestead

his new barn in 1737." —John Adams, diary entry, July 13, 1796

In this version of the event, drawn by a Hamilton supporter, Burr, at left, shoots Hamilton, who fires harmlessly into the air

The Politics of the Pistol

A young nation is shocked by an ancient ritual of honor when Vice President Aaron Burr kills Alexander Hamilton in a **deadly duel**

ALEXANDER HAMILTON AND AARON BURR WERE COMPLI-cated, colorful men whose large talents were almost the equal of their enormous ambitions. And when those ambitions collided on July 11, 1804, atop a rocky ledge in Weehawken, N.J., blood was spilled and two brilliant careers came to an end—although one of the antagonists would not die for another three decades.

Alexander Hamilton still looms large in American life, but the man who killed him, Aaron Burr, remains an enigma. Burr was the son of a respected New Jersey clergyman; his grandfather was Jonathan Edwards, the great Puritan preacher. By age 13, the bright young man was a sophomore at the College of New Jersey (later Princeton University); by 17, he had graduated and taken up the study of law. Burr set aside

his legal ambitions two years later, in 1775, when he enlisted in the Continental Army. Serving under Benedict Arnold in the American assault on Canada, he displayed a gift for guile, disguising himself as a Catholic priest and traveling more than 100 miles behind British lines to deliver an important message. His bravery in two losing battles, at Quebec and Long Island, earned him an officer's commission.

By 1777 both Hamilton and Burr had been appointed to George Washington's personal staff. But while Washington and Hamilton began a lifelong friendship and political partnership, the general didn't take to Burr and soon transferred him to a field command.

After the war, Hamilton became a leader of the Federalists, while Burr sided with the Democratic-Republicans. Yet their

"Adieu, best of wives and best of women. Embrace all my darling children

lives continued to follow a parallel track. Both settled in New York City and embarked on successful legal careers; both were influential in winning support for the new Constitution in 1789. Hamilton became America's first Secretary of the Treasury, while Burr served as a Senator, winning his seat from Hamilton's father-in-law, Philip Schuyler. Burr's victory turned the two men, long rivals, into outright enemies.

When a jealous husband discovered in 1797 that Hamilton was engaged in an affair with his wife, Burr represented Hamilton's mistress, Maria Reynolds, in her divorce proceedings, handing Hamilton a very public humiliation that effectively ended his chances for elective office. In 1800, Burr further hurt his enemy, obtaining and published a scathing broadside that Hamilton had written privately about then U.S. President (and a fellow Federalist) John Adams.

Even with his political career in ruins, Hamilton retained his influence behind the scenes. In the presidential election of 1800, which exposed flaws in the Electoral College by ending in an unexpected tie between allies Thomas Jefferson and Burr, Hamilton lobbied tirelessly—and successfully—for Jefferson. In fact, Hamilton detested Jefferson, but not with the intensity he reserved for Burr. Four years later, with Burr serving as Vice President, Hamilton helped undercut Burr's campaign for the governorship of New York.

Around this time, Hamilton attended a New York dinner party in which he was heard to utter what was later described as "a despicable opinion" about Burr. When accounts of the event were published in newspapers (although exactly what Hamilton said was never specified and remains a mystery), Burr demanded an apology. When Hamilton refused, Burr

Burr, far left, shot and killed Hamilton, below. At left is a letter from Hamilton's daughter Angelica Church, telling her brother about the duel only a few hours after it took place

challenged him to a duel. That Hamilton did not hesitate to accept (even after the death of his son Philip in a duel three years earlier) speaks volumes not only about the era but also about the depth of the hatred these men felt for each other.

The site in New Jersey was chosen because settling disputes with pistols was, by 1804, a serious crime in New York. So on the morning of July 11, the men and their aides rowed across the Hudson to defend their honor. "Both parties took aim and fired in succession," the men's seconds wrote later in a joint statement. Hamilton fired high and wide, shooting into a nearby tree. His supporters would later argue that this was a deliberate attempt to settle the dispute without bloodshed; Burr's partisans would claim it was merely an accident. Burr's aim was sharper. "The pistols were discharged within a few seconds of each other," the aides would remember, "and the fire of Colonel Burr took effect. General Hamilton almost instantly fell." Struck in the stomach, Hamilton was paralyzed from the waist down. Ferried back to New York, he died in agony the following day.

Burr's decline was longer, and perhaps more painful. While Hamilton was mourned as a national hero, the sitting Vice President was indicted for murder in New York and New Jersey, although he was never tried. A few years later, Burr's stillborn scheme to conquer part of the Louisiana Territory and found a new nation, with himself as emperor, led to his trial for treason. Acquitted on a technicality, Burr languished in New York in the years before his death in 1836—destitute, largely forgotten and living under his mother's maiden name lest he be recognized. ■

Artifact

The pistols shown are those used in the duel; they are now the property of the JPMorgan Chase financial firm. At every step in the weeks leading up to the event, the bitter enmity between Hamilton and Burr foiled attempts by their supporters to resolve their grievances without violence. Most duels did not end in death; they were formal rituals that allowed gentlemen to settle matters of honor with an apparent show of bravery, and in many cases, a duelist took care not to shoot directly at his opponent, as Hamilton's seconds claim he did. The deadly outcome in New Jersey led to a national outcry against dueling, and the old custom slowly disappeared.

for me." —Alexander Hamilton to his wife Elizabeth, July 4, 1804

Trinity Churchyard

"What can I do better than withdraw from the Scene? Every day proves to me more and more that this American world was not made for me." —Hamilton

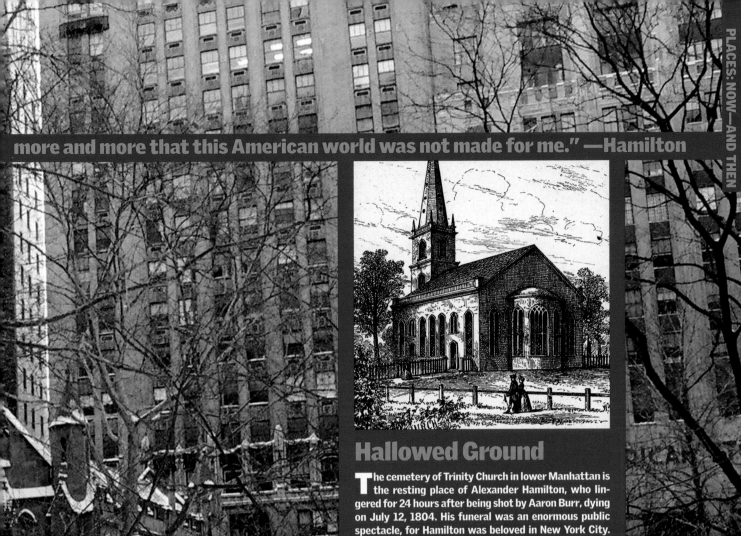

Hallowed Ground

The cemetery of Trinity Church in lower Manhattan is the resting place of Alexander Hamilton, who lingered for 24 hours after being shot by Aaron Burr, dying on July 12, 1804. His funeral was an enormous public spectacle, for Hamilton was beloved in New York City. While the cemetery where he rests is unchanged, this is the third Trinity Church to occupy this ground; the second church, from his day, is shown in the etching above.

In addition to its links to Hamilton, this old churchyard evokes a nearly forgotten era of American history, when New York City was the nation's capital. A few minutes' walk away is Federal Hall, the first seat of the new government formed under the Constitution of 1787; it was here that George Washington was sworn in as the first President on April 30, 1789, following his unanimous election by the 69 delegates to the first Electoral College. Under the terms of the Residence Act of 1790, however, the capital was relocated to a new Federal District to be carved out of Virginia and Maryland. Philadelphia was designated the temporary capital, and Independence Hall became the seat of government from 1790 to 1800.

Trinity churchyard is also a moment's walk from Wall Street. In building Washington, the U.S. deliberately divided its political and financial centers. Although New York City lost its chance to become the nation's capital, it has remained its greatest city. The building of the Erie Canal ensured its position as a key port, and in a later era the city became the chief portal for European immigrants, a role symbolized by the great Statue of Liberty in its harbor. In 2001 Trinity Churchyard again entered history: located three short blocks from the World Trade Center, the churchyard was cloaked in ash when the Twin Towers fell. Its sister church, St. Paul's Chapel, where Washington knelt in prayer after his Inauguration, is directly across the street from the Trade Center; it became a primary support facility for the rescue workers of ground zero. ∎

THE OLD JOKE ABOUT WASHINGTON, D.C., IS THAT THE city boasts the ideal combination of Southern efficiency and Northern charm. The easy stereotype taps into a difficult truth: the location of the nation's capital city was precisely chosen, brokered in a political bargain that barely preserved the frail young union. Americans were inventing a nation from scratch, and now they decided to create the seat of the Federal Government in the same manner. Clearly, naming an existing city the nation's capital would amount to declaring its home state the first among equals in the union—and the union was already imperiled by the rivalries between large and small states, Northern and Southern states.

So a new city must be built—but where? The issue of the capital's location soon became entangled with another dilemma roiling the union: the debts incurred by the states in fighting the Revolution. Who was to pay them? The Northern states wanted the Federal Government to assume the debts; the Southern states, wary of conceding too much power to the federal

"No nation perhaps had ever before the opportunity ... of deliberately deciding

Inventing a Capital City

Its location is a bargaining chip, and George Washington fires its first architect. Yet the **Federal City** rises, with an eye trained on the future

The U.S. Capitol, sans dome, rises atop Jenkins Hill in this watercolor by William Burch, painted circa 1800

union, preferred to assume the Revolution's debts themselves.

At a dinner meeting in June 1790, Virginians Thomas Jefferson and James Madison hammered out a bargain with New Yorker Alexander Hamilton: the union would assume the war debts, and the nation's new capital would be located in a new federal district on the Potomac River to be carved out of two Southern states, Virginia and Maryland, not far from the new President's home.

The unspoken subtext of the agreement—a subject that was often not addressed in formal assemblies but was ever present in the tense relationship between the states—was the preservation of slavery. The location of the Federal City in a new District of Columbia straddling two of the nation's largest slave states was ratified in the Residence Act of 1790, and it amounted to a tacit agreement by the Northern states that slavery would be allowed to continue in the South. It was the first of three major compromises that would occur in exact 30-year intervals—the Compromise of 1790, the Missouri Compromise of

where their Capital City should be fixed." —Pierre L'Enfant

Artifacts

Pierre L'Enfant's plan for the design of the capital city, above, calls for a standard right-angle street grid intersected by broad avenues arrayed in diagonals. More than 200 years later, the plan can be seen in the inset picture at right, which shows the U.S. Capitol building, with L'Enfant's avenues radiating out from it. Setting the White House and Capitol building in opposition, L'Enfant's plan mirrored the checks and balances written into the Constitution, although it slighted the Supreme Court, which received neither a fine home nor a connecting avenue and vista. The court did not receive its own building until 1935.

MPI—GETTY IMAGES; INSETS: LEFT, TIME LIFE PICTURE COLLECTION; RIGHT: ROYALTY-FREE—CORBIS

1820, the Compromise of 1850—that would preserve the union at the expense of continuing the "peculiar institution" so essential to the nation's economy.

WHATEVER ITS POLITICAL GENESIS, THE DECISION TO create a capital from scratch presented the young nation with a mighty opportunity: the chance to construct in stone a city equal to the far-reaching visions of the country's founders. And George Washington knew just the right man for the job: Major Pierre Charles L'Enfant, who had served under the general in the war. In a 1789 letter to the new President, the French artist and architect described his vision of such a city: "The plan should be drawn on such a scale as to leave room for the aggrandisement & embellishment which the increase of the wealth of the Nation will permit it to pursue at any period how ever remote."

Washington hired L'Enfant, who set to work laying out a grid for the new Federal City, a 100-sq.-mi. plot along the Potomac. His design featured a standard grid of streets, with a promising twist: broad avenues would dissect the grid at diagonals, converging in traffic circles and creating a series of dramatic, lengthy vistas. The plan's two most dominant buildings would be erected on the focal points of the terrain: a "Congress House" on the area's highest point, Jenkins Hill, and a "President's Palace" some 1.5 miles away, also on a hill. The two would be connected by one of L'Enfant's 160-ft.-wide avenues.

Sadly, L'Enfant disappointed his old commander; he proved ineffectual and had to be dismissed in 1792. The surveying and plotting of the new city were completed by civil engineer Andrew Ellicott, assisted by the African-American mathematical genius Benjamin Banneker. With L'Enfant out of the picture, the government held a competition to design the Capitol building, and the $500 prize was won by a Scottish physician, William Thornton. His plan called for an immense building with two rectangular wings connected by a central dome. A later architect, Benjamin Latrobe, scaled down the size of the building, but with more than 500 rooms, it remains immense. The structure was long in construction; its great dome was still taking shape during the Civil War.

As for L'Enfant's "President's Palace," republican sentiment rechristened it the Executive Mansion, and after it was built, it came to be called the White House, just as the Federal City was christened Washington, D.C., after the first President's death. L'Enfant's original idea called for a palatial structure five times bigger than the one that was finally built; but with Thomas Jefferson and others urging restraint, a scaled-down design created by Irish architect James Hoban prevailed. George Washington, ever the commander, bullied its construction through. Early on, the District of Columbia Commissioners shut down a brothel operating among the shacks of the workers building the mansion. Vehement protest from carpenters and stone carvers produced yet another compromise; the establishment was allowed to reopen discreetly in another part of the raw town.

John Adams was the first President to occupy the structure; he moved into the unfinished home early in 1801, during the last three months of his term. Alone on his second night, writing a letter to Abigail, he pondered the fate of the new dwelling and its future occupants. "I pray heaven to bestow the best of blessings on this house and on all that shall hereafter inhabit it," he wrote. "May none but honest and wise men ever rule under this roof." Franklin Roosevelt had the words carved in the marble mantel of the State Dining Room 145 years later, and Adams' powerful words still resonate in American hearts. ■

This drawing of the White House dates to 1807, seven years before the British burned the building in the War of 1812

The Lewis and Clark company explores the Columbia River, 1805

Heading West

Expansion: 1775-1828

1775
Daniel Boone opens Cumberland Gap

1787
The Northwest Ordinance is adopted

1794
U.S. Army defeats Indian confederation at the Battle of Fallen Timbers

1797
Johnny Appleseed begins travels

1801
Second Great Awakening, religious revival, begins in Kentucky

1803
Louisiana Purchase signed; John J. Audubon comes to America

1804
Lewis and Clark Expedition sets off on journey of Western discovery

1806
Lewis and Clark Expedition returns

1811
William H. Harrison defeats Tecumseh's Indian confederation at Tippecanoe

1812
War of 1812 begins

1813
Battle of the Thames River; Tecumseh is defeated and dies

1814
Andrew Jackson defeats Creek tribes in Southeastern territories

1815
Building of Cumberland Road begins

1819
Spain relinquishes Florida to U.S.

1820
Daniel Boone dies in Missouri

1827
Audubon publishes *Birds of America*

The Pathfinder

MASS MOVEMENTS RELY ON FIGUREHEADS, AND American culture brims with larger-than-life personifications of its dreams and desires. Two centuries ago, when the wilderness still needed taming, and restless Americans first embraced the westering urge and began lighting out for the territories, Daniel Boone became the icon of the frontier. And there he remains. Hubert Humphrey once said, "There is in every American, I think, something of the old Daniel Boone—who, when he could see the smoke from another chimney, felt himself too crowded and moved further out into the wilderness."

Born in 1734 in the western reaches of Pennsylvania, Boone had little formal education but displayed an early talent for hunting and exploring. In his 20s, Boone joined expeditions to seize Fort Duquesne (now Pittsburgh) during the French and Indian War. By the time he was 35, Boone had blazed the first trail between North Carolina and Tennessee. In 1775, he led a party of 30 woodsmen who cut, marked and mapped the Wilderness Road, a 300-mile-long network of trails that led from Virginia, North Carolina and Pennsylvania through the Cumberland Gap and into Kentucky, a feat that made him an American Moses, leading his people to the Promised Land.

It was in Kentucky, which he almost singlehandedly opened to settlement, that Boone's reputation would take on the status of myth. It was there that he was captured by Shawnee Indians, then adopted as a son by their chief, Blackfish, only to escape after five months so that he could warn rebel settlers of an impending attack by Native Americans and their British allies. Boone's growing legend would be helped along by his gift for sound bites. "I have never been lost," he once said, "but I will admit to being confused for several weeks." Why was he leaving sparsely settled Kentucky for wilder territory in Missouri? "Too crowded." Soon his exploits began showing up in the mass media of his day: an admiring biography, *The Adventures of Colonel Daniel Boone*, appeared in 1782; even Lord Byron extolled Boone's courage in *Don Juan*.

In later years, Boone himself seems to have been taken aback by all the fuss. Before his death in 1820, he would reflect that "with me the world has taken great liberties, and yet I have been but a common man." Ironically—or perhaps intentionally—such "aw-shucks" protestations only further cemented Boone's grip on the imagination of a thoroughly entranced public. ■

"Many heroic exploits and chivalrous adventures are related to me which

Boone looks older than his age, 36, in this 1770 portrait. He would live for 50 more years

Daniel Boone

exist only in the regions of fancy ... I have been but a common man."

ILLUSTRATION FOR TIME BY DUGALD STERMER

Sacagawea

"Sacagawea ... sat down, and was beginning to interpret, when ... she recognised her brother. She instantly jumped up, and ran and embraced him."—Lewis and Clark, *Journals*

Wilderness Guide

BORN INTO THE SHOSHONE TRIBE IN MONTANA IN THE late 1780s or early '90s, Sacagawea was kidnapped by a raiding party from the rival Hidatsa tribe around 1800 and spirited away as a slave to North Dakota. Her captors sold her to a French trader, Toussaint Charbonneau, who, with his pregnant teenage "wife," joined Lewis and Clark's expedition at its first winter camp in 1804. The explorers groused that a young woman about to give birth could hardly be expected to endure the hardships ahead, but they reconsidered upon learning that she knew the land and language of the Shoshone.

One Indian tribe after another was initially startled by the appearance of a heavily armed party of whites deep within their homelands, but each was reassured by the presence of a Native American mother and child that the explorers had come in peace; they would otherwise almost certainly have been slaughtered. As the trek progressed, Sacagawea ("Janey" to Clark) became so essential that when she fell ill in Montana, Lewis confided to his diary that "if this woman dies, our mission may fail."

Happily, Sacagawea lived, the mission succeeded, and Lewis and Clark were hailed as heroes. Lost amid the fanfare was the role of the indispensable woman who had carried her newborn son up and down mountains and across swift rivers, earning nothing for her trouble, so that a new nation could take the measure of itself. ∎

Johnny Appleseed

"His dress was ... cast-off clothing, taken in payment for apple trees." —*Harper's*, 1871

Food for Thought

IT'S GOOD TO BE KING, EVEN BETTER TO BE A FOLK HERO. Untethered from the nagging confines of fact, one's legend floats free, growing and changing, yet always reflecting the culture whose dreams and visions it attracts. John Chapman, a.k.a. Johnny Appleseed, is one such type. He's a magnet for our aspirations, and while it is true that most of the exploits attributed to him are mere folklore, it is also true that there is nothing "mere" about folklore.

Here is what we know for sure about Chapman. He was born in 1774 in Leominster, Mass. He became a nurseryman and traveled to the Northwest Territory, joining in the great migration that brought settlers to the future states of Ohio, Indiana, Michigan and Illinois. He specialized in cultivating and selling apple trees. He died in 1845. Twenty-six years later, an article in *Harper's* magazine by W.D. Haley first brought his name before the larger public; it

was the founding moment of the Appleseed legend.

Here is what we can't confirm about Chapman but like to believe is true: he had a vision, in which he saw America's Western lands filling with apple blossoms, and he became a pilgrim of horticulture, traveling barefoot across the territories proffering apple seeds and saplings free to all he encountered. He befriended the Indians—this is important—and some say he preached religion, favoring the teachings of the Swedish mystic Emanuel Swedenborg. Part Yankee peddler, part St. Francis of Assisi, Chapman is pictured with a cooking pot on his head and sleeping with friendly beasts. How much of this fable is fact? We may never know—but it's a fact that we need our folk heroes, and to admire a man whose image embraces horticulture, charity, tolerance, spiritual yearning and the love of nature is about as American as ... well, you know what. ∎

Many Tribes, One People

ON THESE PAGES, AS IN HIS LIFE AND DEATH, TECUMSEH, THE mighty Shawnee warrior, is paired with his great nemesis, William Henry Harrison. "Tippecanoe" Harrison would ride his victories over the Indian chief all the way to the White House in 1840; how shocked he would be to learn that almost 200 years after he and Tecumseh battled along the western frontier, it is the Native American, not the white general, who is widely considered the greater man of the two.

Tecumseh, Pontiac's heir, is one of a long series of Indian heroes whose lives follow a similar, tragic trajectory: recoiling at the greed and guile of the settlers, they take up arms, preach a return to the old ways of the fathers, unite diverse tribes to fight the white encroachers—and then are brutally overwhelmed by the superior numbers and technology of the Europeans.

Tecumseh's partner in his lost cause was his brother, Tenskwatawa, known as the Prophet, who adressed the spiritual aspects of the struggle. The two set up a village dedicated to their new way of life, which rejected alcohol and other white habits, at Deer Creek in the Indiana Territory in 1795. Here the brothers called for a confederation of tribes, hoping to stop the whites from playing the Indians off against each other. As their influence spread, a confrontation loomed: finally, Harrison beat the Prophet at Tippecanoe in 1811; two years later, at the Battle of the Thames, his troops killed both Tecumseh and his dream. ■

Tecumseh

"We are determined to defend our lands ... we wish to leave our bones upon them."

Indian Fighter

WHEN WILLIAM HENRY HARRISON RAN for the presidency in 1840, with John Tyler of Tennessee as his running mate, his astute political handlers coined the first, and one of the most memorable, of American campaign slogans: "Tippecanoe and Tyler too!" Never mind that the Battle of Tippecanoe was by then a relic from the distant past, fought 29 years before; and never mind that the glorious victory that earned Harrison his handle amounted to a narrow win over the confederation of tribes put together by the great Shawnee chief Tecumseh.

Harrison's entire life was obscured in the 1840 race; although he was portrayed as a roughhewn son of the frontier, born in a log cabin, he was in fact a descendant of Virginia aristocracy: his father Benjamin had signed the Declaration of Independence. Born in 1773, Harrison headed west as a young man, bearing a commission from George Washington to fight the Indians along the frontier. He served under General Anthony Wayne at the Battle of Fallen Timbers, which opened the Ohio Valley to white settlers, then, at only 27, he was named Governor of the new Territory of Indiana, putting him in the front lines of the constant friction between white settlers and native tribes. At first, aware of the injustices visited by the Americans on the Indians, he hoped to serve as an ambassador between the two races, but he soon was actively devising successful plans to woo the Native Americans from their lands. In 1810, Tecumseh came to the governor's mansion, Grouseland, and declared that the Indians would yield no more land. His vow flared into rebellion at Tippecanoe in 1811, but the confederation died, with Tecumseh, at the Battle of the Thames two years later.

"Tippecanoe" won his race for the White House in 1840. He gave the longest Inaugural Address in history, caught a cold from delivering it on a raw, windy day and died a month later, the first President to die in office. As the British say, his political career was a long run—for a short slide. ∎

William Henry Harrison

"In the course of seven years the Indian title was extinguished [by] fifty millions of acres."

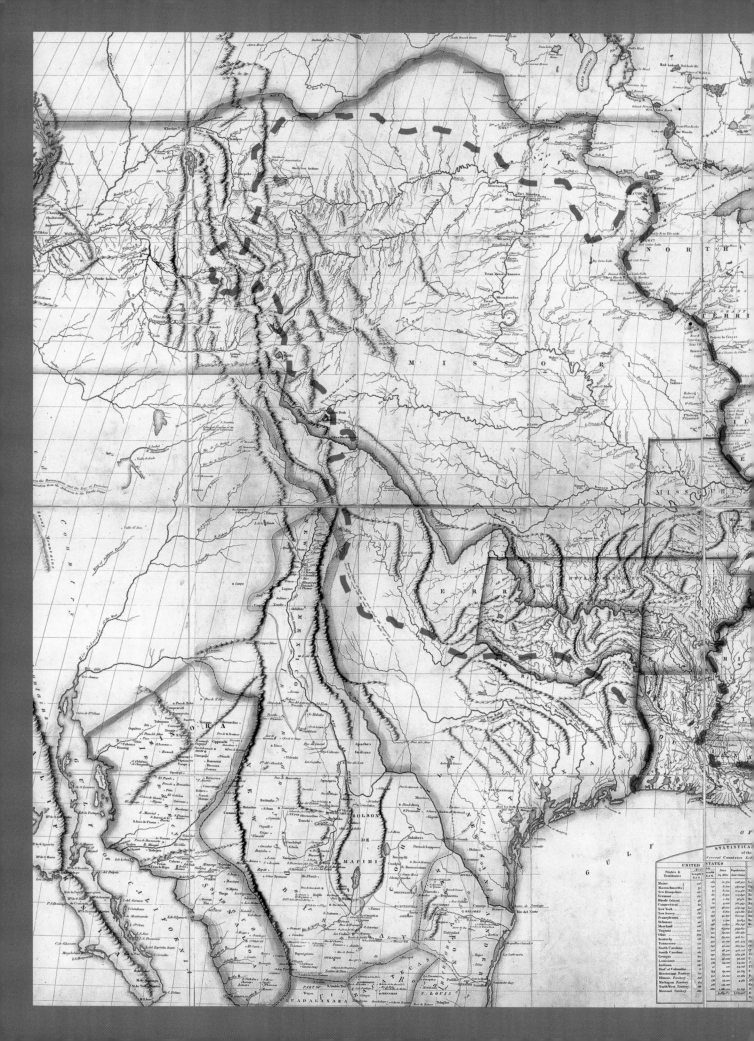

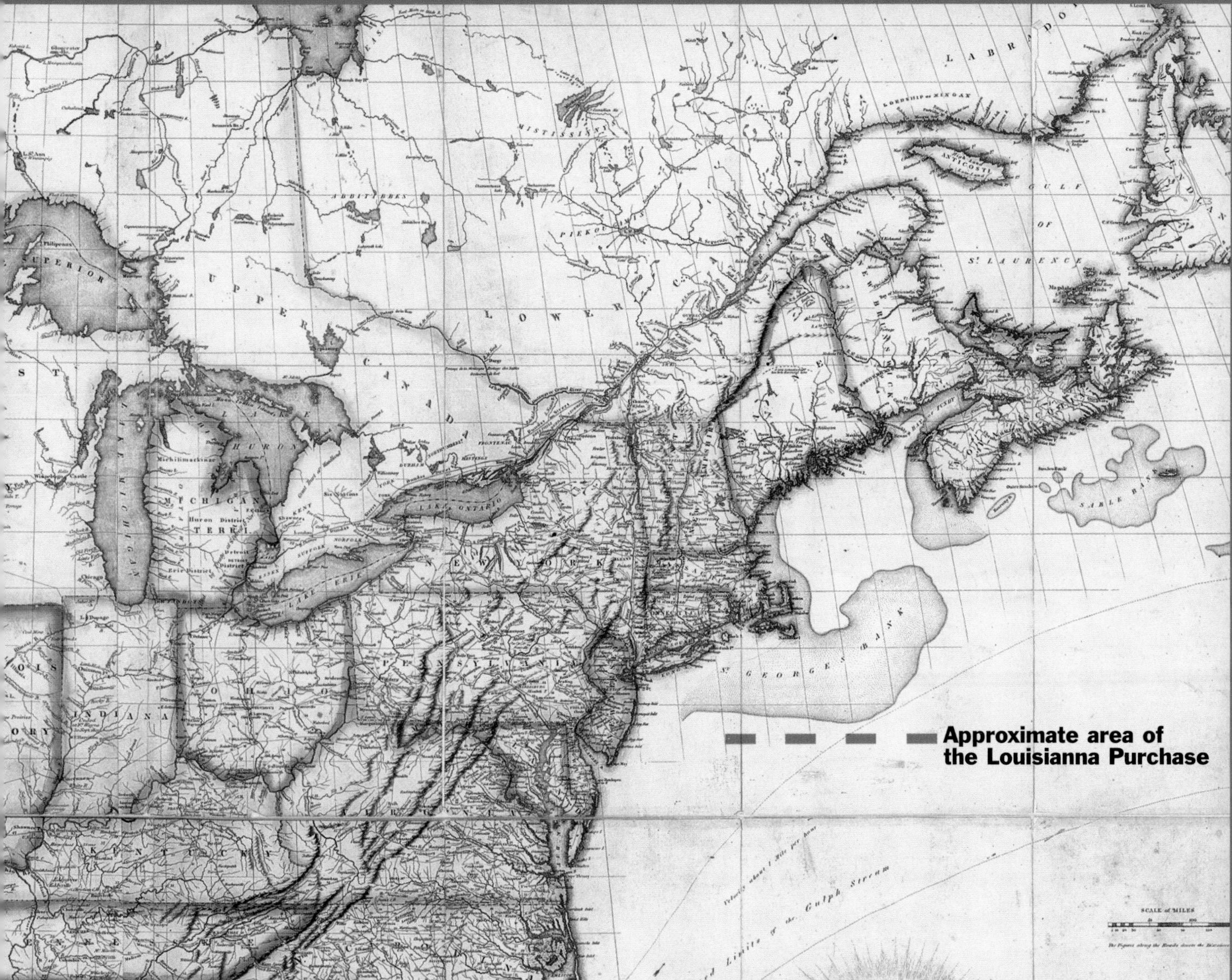

- - - - - **Approximate area of
the Louisianna Purchase**

SCALE of MILES

How the West Was Won

Louisiana
Purchase

The Louisiana Purchase may well be history's greatest real-estate
bargain ($24 for Manhattan isn't bad, either). The deal resulted from
the changing priorities of two European colonial powers, Spain and France.
Spain had long held claim to the land but lacked the resources to develop it,
and title to the sweeping prairies and soaring mountains of the American
West was passed, secretly, to France's energetic ruler, Napoleon Bonaparte, in 1800. When President Thomas Jefferson heard of this, he sent
Secretary of State James Monroe to France, asking if the U.S. could buy
West Florida and New Orleans for $2 million. Monroe got a much better
deal—800,000 sq. mi. of the West. Jefferson had qualms, but he also had
vision. He leaped at the chance to create a continental destiny for the U.S.

Lewis, left, and Clark acted as equals but had different temperaments. The inset at right is a page from one of the journals of the Corps

Across the Wide Missouri

Boldly going where few white men had gone before, the explorers of the **Lewis & Clark Expedition** helped chart the nation's continental destiny

THOMAS JEFFERSON HAD A PROBLEM: HE HAD COMPLETED one of history's great land transactions, buying 800,000 sq. mi. of the American West from Napoleon Bonaparte. Yet the third President had no idea whether he had purchased a pig in a poke or a paradise. Very few Europeans had traversed the vast lands between the Mississippi River and the Pacific Ocean. A few fur trappers had wandered its rivers and mountains, but their tales were an unscientific mishmash concocted of moonshine and secondhand Native American lore. An expedition must be mounted, to answer a thousand questions: Where was the fabled Northwest Passage, the transcontinental route to the sea? How many Indians lived in the West, in how many tribes, and how did they view the white man? What sorts of new plants, new birds, new animals might be found there? It was all catnip for Jefferson, a great man of the Enlightenment: a chance to play Adam in a new Eden, but an Adam with all the latest tools of modern science—after all, this was the 19th century! He picked his aide Meriwether Lewis to lead the Corps of Discovery, and Lewis then asked his friend William Clark to join him on the great journey.

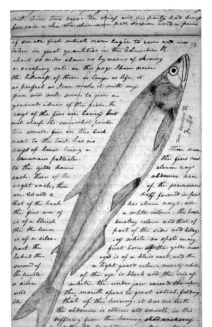

Historians traditionally distinguish the two by contrasting their personalities—the brooding Lewis played off against the genial Clark—Jeremy Irons hitting the road with John Goodman. Gary Moulton, editor of the explorers' journals, says, "The differences existed, but they may have been exaggerated." In reality, the two men had a great deal in common. They were both Virginians. They were both Army officers, six-footers and experienced outdoorsmen, who first met eight years before the expedition, when they were serving in Indian campaigns in the Ohio Valley. They shared with Jefferson a passion for such Enlightenment sciences as ethnology, paleontology, zoology and botany, and sent him specimens from their trek, which he displayed at Monticello.

Older than Lewis by four years—Clark was 33 and Lewis 29 when the expedition began—Clark was the more experienced soldier and frontiersman. His five older brothers had fought in the American Revolution. One, General George Rogers Clark, had led raids that kept the lower Great Lakes region out of British hands. As an Army officer, William had trekked the Ohio Valley, leading troops at least once in a skir-

mish with Indians. But by 1803 George was sinking into alcoholism, and William had resigned his commission in part to help settle his brother's debts. The two were living together on a point of land overlooking the Ohio River just below Louisville when William received an astonishing letter from his old Army buddy.

For the previous two years, Lewis had been working in the White House as Jefferson's private secretary. Like Jefferson, Lewis had lost his father at an early age; now he was in daily contact with the President, who was practically a surrogate father to him. Lewis wrote Clark that Jefferson had placed him in charge of a mission to explore "the interior of the continent of North America, or that part of it bordering on the Missourie & Columbia Rivers." Moreover, Lewis wanted Clark to be his co-commander. Leaving George in his family's care, William accepted "chearfully," and "with much pleasure."

The explorers embarked from St. Louis, then the last outpost of U.S. influence in the West, on May 14, 1804, leading 23 young, rawboned frontiersmen into the wilderness. The party included Clark's slave York, a huge black man whose color would fascinate the Indians. After five months of battling upstream along the Missouri River, the company made winter camp near what is now the city of Bismarck, N.D. Here an important couple joined the party: the French-Canadian voyageur Toussaint Charbonneau and his wife Sacagawea, a 17-year-old Shoshone who spoke some of the language of the mountain tribes and, more important, knew some of the terrain ahead. In fact, the young woman's guidance would prove invaluable. She gave birth to a boy, Pomp, before the snows melted; the men broke camp and moved west again on April 7, 1805.

The party passed across the Great Plains, dining on buffalo meat, encountering and receiving the aid of the Shoshone, crossing the mountain ranges and dipping their canteens into the Salmon, the Snake and the Columbia rivers, then building canoes to carry them down the Columbia to the Pacific. On Nov. 15, they first saw the great ocean. They roughed it through a rugged winter on the Northwest coast, then turned themselves around and set their sights on the sunrise the next spring. On Sept. 23, 1806, after 28 months of hardship and wonder, they reached St. Louis. Congress

Fantastic Voyage

With their small flotilla heading up the Missouri, Lewis and Clark expected to find an easy water pathway to the Pacific but found the Rockies instead. Nothing they had ever seen before prepared them for the hardships they would face

GRAPHIC BY LON TWEETEN • TEXT BY JACKSON DYKMAN

The Red Pirogue

Lewis bought it, possibly in Pittsburgh, to lighten the keelboat's load on the shallow Ohio River. The 41-ft. craft was hidden with supplies at the Marias River in what is now Montana. Returning 13 months later, the men found the boat had rotted away

Crew of up to eight

Up to 9 tons of cargo

Flat bottom

THE BOATS

The corps used 25 vessels throughout the journey. A 26th boat— a custom-designed collapsible iron frame covered with skins—was carried all the way to what is now Montana, where it failed upon hitting the water

Before setting out, Lewis bought $33 worth of "flagg stuff." At the time, the U.S. flag had 15 stars and stripes

Retractable roof

Crew of up to 27

The Keelboat

Lewis designed the craft and oversaw its often delayed construction in Pittsburgh. This largest craft of the expedition never made it past what is now North Dakota. In spring of 1805, it returned to St. Louis, carrying men, specimens and reports

Carried perhaps 12 tons of cargo and, when loaded, drew 3 ft. to 4 ft. of water

Cabin

55 ft. long

8 ft. wide

Crews of four to six

Dugout Canoes

The crew carved 15 canoes by hand during its journey—and carried some of them on crude wagons for 17 miles around the Great Falls of the Missouri. Empty, each weighed more than a ton

Two canoes could be tied together to form a catamaran

Some were about 30 ft. long

2 to 3 tons of cargo capacity

It took 16 men a month to carve their first six canoes from felled trees. Near the trip's end, the men made two canoes in just three days

TOOLS OF THE TRIP

Producing an accurate map was imperative. The **compass** was crucial to navigation and surveying

Beads were a primary currency of trade with the Indians. When the explorers ran out of beads, they used buttons cut from their coats

Lewis and Clark gave **the Jefferson Peace Medal** to Indian chiefs they met as a symbol of friendship from their new "chief" in Washington

A 32-ft. mast held a large square sail and a foresail; the mast was hinged at the bottom so it could be lowered

In addition to rowing, crewmen could move the boat by pushing poles into the river's bottom

As many as 12 poles or 22 oars at a time

Locker lids formed a walkway for poling

Men or horses sometimes used ropes to pull the boats from shore or from the water

Hemp towline

Square sail and sprit sail

Crew of up to six

Oarsmen's benches

Up to 8 tons of cargo

The White Pirogue

This smallest boat to leave was the largest craft to return two years later. Originally slated to carry provisions, it became the officers' boat, carrying the most vital instruments and supplies

About 35 ft. long

Made of poplar, probably painted white

Flat bottom

Retractable awning

Waterfowl fly through a dawn mist on the Beaverhead River near Dillon, Montana, where Sacagawea led Lewis and Clark in 1805

rewarded the two leaders with 1,600 acres of land each; the troops received 320 acres each and double pay.

Lewis and Clark got along well from the start, divvying up their responsibilities: Clark was the better boatman and navigator; Lewis, the planner and natural historian, often walked ashore collecting specimens. Clark had the cooler head. He brokered a crucial early compromise that ended a staredown with the Teton Sioux. The more mercurial Lewis hurled a puppy into the face of an Indian who angered him, and killed a Blackfeet in the corps's only violent incident.

Nothing reveals the captains more than their treatment of Sacagawea. Lewis could be aloof, dismissing her as "the Indian woman," observing that "if she has enough to eat and a few trinkets to wear I believe she would be perfectly content anywhere." But the less formal Clark nicknamed her "Janey" and treated her warmly. She repaid him with gifts, including "two Dozen white weazils tails" on Christmas Day 1805.

WE KNOW THESE DETAILS BECAUSE LEWIS AND CLARK kept scrupulously complete journals—13 volumes of them. We can look over their shoulders as they and their party contend with hunger, disease, blizzards, broiling sun, boiling rapids, furious grizzly bears and unrelenting plagues of tormenting "musquetors." We know about the Indians who helped them, and we know that they had to eat dogs and horses to survive. We are in the canoe with Clark when he writes, "Ocian in view! O! the joy," straining to hear the waves breaking on the shore he had sought for so long.

The last task of the voyage—publishing their account—fell to Lewis. He had kept the raw notes and journals he and Clark had painstakingly carried to the Pacific and back with the goal of editing them into final form. But unsteady in his new job as Governor of Louisiana Territory, frustrated in his romantic aspirations and sinking into a depression fueled by alcohol and possibly disease, Lewis developed writer's block. He died in 1809; the cause is still hotly debated, although most historians believe it was suicide.

Clark took over the project, and the journals finally came out in a two-volume edition in 1814 that left out most of the expedition's significant scientific discoveries. What it did include was a cartographic masterpiece: Clark's map of the West. For the first time the blank spaces on the continent had been filled in with generally accurate representations of mountain ranges and rivers. Prominently marked on Clark's map were the names of dozens of tribes that lived there, in bold type that continues to undermine the notion that the West was ever an unpopulated wilderness.

The press run was a paltry 1,417 copies. It sold poorly. Two years later, Clark still had not received his own copy. No matter: 200 years and hundreds of books later, it's hard to imagine the absence of Lewis and Clark from the pageant of popular American history. The country they returned through was not the the same country they had just crossed. Its rivers had been named, its plants and animals sketched and classified, its native peoples apprised of their new status as subjects of a distant government whose claim to the place consisted of a document, the Louisiana Purchase, that none of its actual inhabitants had signed. For better and for worse—the latter would be the fate of the natives—America's vision of itself now stretched from sea to shining sea. ■

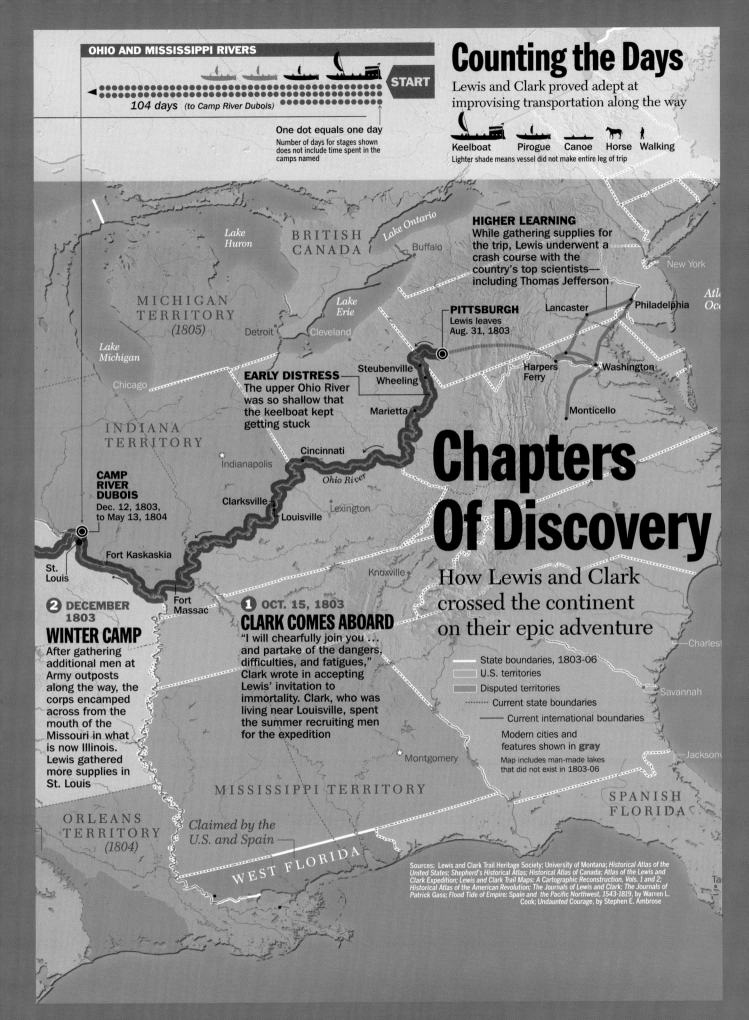

OHIO AND MISSISSIPPI RIVERS

START

104 days (to Camp River Dubois)

One dot equals one day
Number of days for stages shown
does not include time spent in the
camps named

Counting the Days

Lewis and Clark proved adept at
improvising transportation along the way

Keelboat   Pirogue   Canoe   Horse   Walking

Lighter shade means vessel did not make entire leg of trip

HIGHER LEARNING
While gathering supplies for
the trip, Lewis underwent a
crash course with the
country's top scientists—
including Thomas Jefferson

PITTSBURGH
Lewis leaves
Aug. 31, 1803

EARLY DISTRESS
The upper Ohio River
was so shallow that
the keelboat kept
getting stuck

CAMP RIVER DUBOIS
Dec. 12, 1803,
to May 13, 1804

Chapters Of Discovery

How Lewis and Clark
crossed the continent
on their epic adventure

State boundaries, 1803-06
U.S. territories
Disputed territories
Current state boundaries
Current international boundaries

Modern cities and
features shown in gray
Map includes man-made lakes
that did not exist in 1803-06

2 DECEMBER 1803

WINTER CAMP

After gathering
additional men at
Army outposts
along the way, the
corps encamped
across from the
mouth of the
Missouri in what
is now Illinois.
Lewis gathered
more supplies in
St. Louis

1 OCT. 15, 1803

CLARK COMES ABOARD

"I will chearfully join you …
and partake of the dangers,
difficulties, and fatigues,"
Clark wrote in accepting
Lewis' invitation to
immortality. Clark, who was
living near Louisville, spent
the summer recruiting men
for the expedition

Claimed by the
U.S. and Spain

Lake Huron

BRITISH CANADA

Lake Ontario
Buffalo

Lake Erie

New York

Atl
Oc

MICHIGAN TERRITORY
(1805)

Detroit   Cleveland

Lake Michigan

Chicago

Steubenville
Wheeling

Lancaster   Philadelphia

Harpers Ferry   Washington

Marietta

Monticello

INDIANA TERRITORY

Cincinnati

Indianapolis   Ohio River

Clarksville

Louisville   Lexington

Knoxville

St. Louis

Fort Kaskaskia

Fort Massac

Charles

Savannah

Jackson

Montgomery

MISSISSIPPI TERRITORY

SPANISH FLORIDA

ORLEANS TERRITORY
(1804)

WEST FLORIDA

Ta

Sources: Lewis and Clark Trail Heritage Society; University of Montana; Historical Atlas of the
United States; Shepherd's Historical Atlas; Historical Atlas of Canada; Atlas of the Lewis and
Clark Expedition; Lewis and Clark Trail Maps: A Cartographic Reconstruction, Vols. 1 and 2;
Historical Atlas of the American Revolution; The Journals of Lewis and Clark; The Journals of
Patrick Gass; Flood Tide of Empire: Spain and the Pacific Northwest, 1543-1819, by Warren L.
Cook; Undaunted Courage, by Stephen E. Ambrose

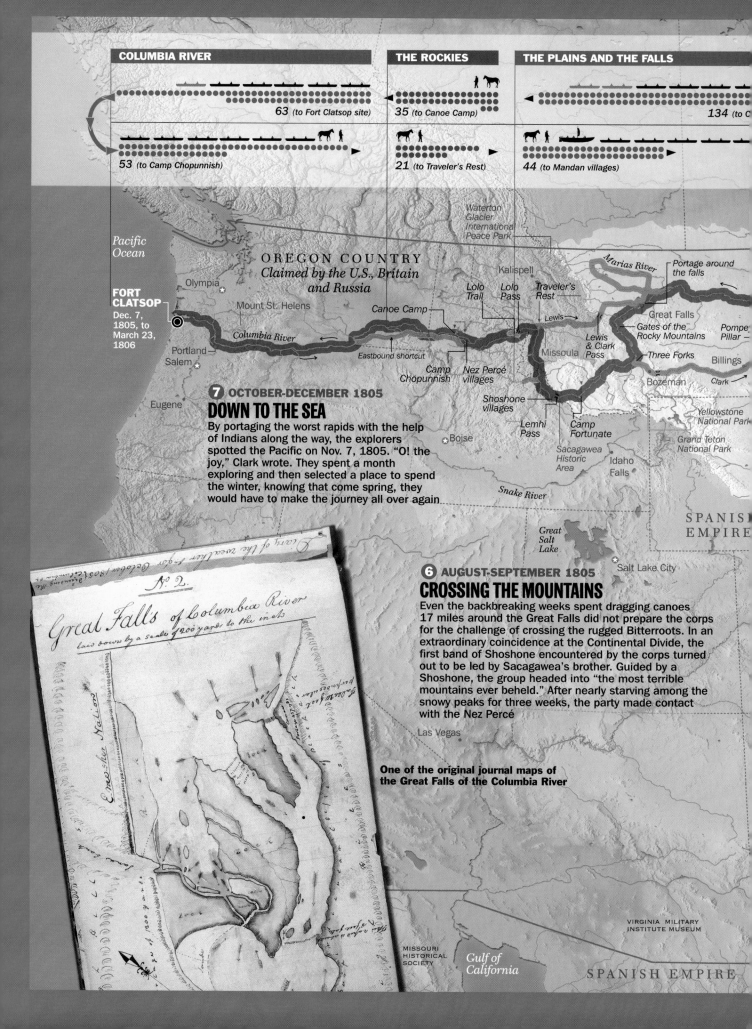

COLUMBIA RIVER

63 (to Fort Clatsop site)

53 (to Camp Chopunnish)

THE ROCKIES

35 (to Canoe Camp)

21 (to Traveler's Rest)

THE PLAINS AND THE FALLS

134 (to C

44 (to Mandan villages)

Pacific
Ocean

FORT CLATSOP
Dec. 7, 1805, to March 23, 1806

Olympia

OREGON COUNTRY
Claimed by the U.S., Britain and Russia

Mount St. Helens

Columbia River

Portland
Salem

Eugene

Boise

Kalispell

Waterton Glacier International Peace Park

Lolo Trail
Lolo Pass
Canoe Camp
Eastbound shortcut
Camp Chopunnish
Nez Percé villages

Traveler's Rest
Lewis
Missoula
Lewis & Clark Pass

Shoshone villages
Lemhi Pass
Camp Fortunate
Sacagawea Historic Area
Idaho Falls

Snake River

Marias River
Portage around the falls
Great Falls
Gates of the Rocky Mountains
Three Forks

Bozeman

Pompe
Pillar

Billings

Clark

Yellowstone National Park

Grand Teton National Park

Great Salt Lake

Salt Lake City

Las Vegas

SPANISH
EMPIRE

7 OCTOBER-DECEMBER 1805

DOWN TO THE SEA

By portaging the worst rapids with the help of Indians along the way, the explorers spotted the Pacific on Nov. 7, 1805. "O! the joy," Clark wrote. They spent a month exploring and then selected a place to spend the winter, knowing that come spring, they would have to make the journey all over again

6 AUGUST-SEPTEMBER 1805

CROSSING THE MOUNTAINS

Even the backbreaking weeks spent dragging canoes 17 miles around the Great Falls did not prepare the corps for the challenge of crossing the rugged Bitterroots. In an extraordinary coincidence at the Continental Divide, the first band of Shoshone encountered by the corps turned out to be led by Sacagawea's brother. Guided by a Shoshone, the group headed into "the most terrible mountains ever beheld." After nearly starving among the snowy peaks for three weeks, the party made contact with the Nez Percé

One of the original journal maps of the Great Falls of the Columbia River

Great Falls of Columbia River
laid down by a scale of 200 yards to the inch

No. 2.

Enesher Nation

VIRGINIA MILITARY
INSTITUTE MUSEUM

MISSOURI
HISTORICAL
SOCIETY

Gulf of California

SPANISH EMPIRE

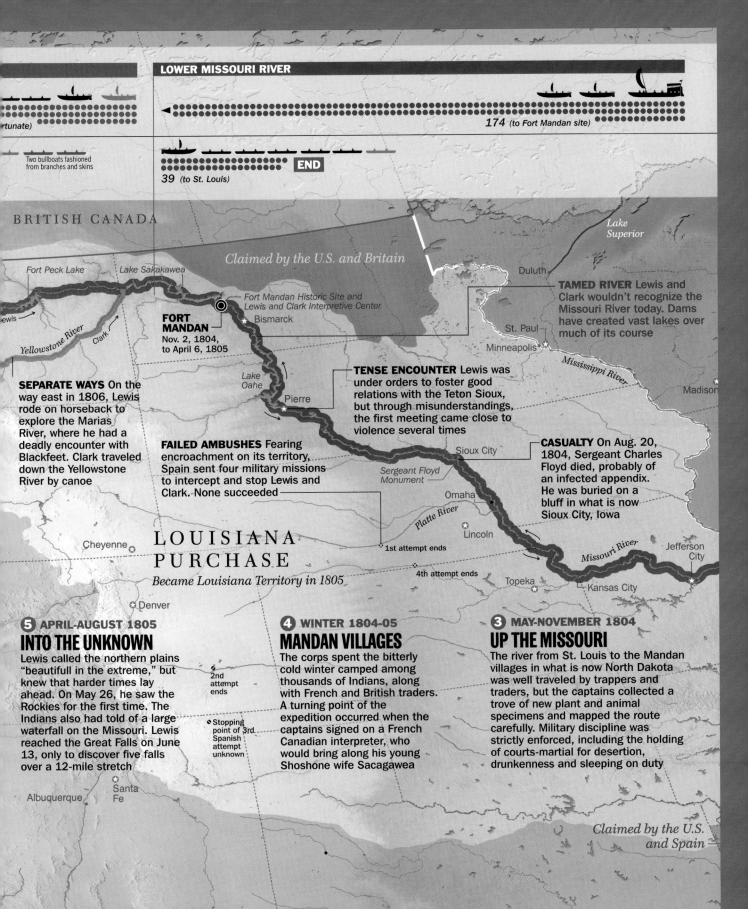

...tunate)

174 (to Fort Mandan site)

Two bullboats fashioned
from branches and skins

END

39 (to St. Louis)

BRITISH CANADA

Lake Superior

Fort Peck Lake

Lake Sakakawea

...ewis →

Duluth

TAMED RIVER Lewis and Clark wouldn't recognize the Missouri River today. Dams have created vast lakes over much of its course

Yellowstone River → Clark →

Fort Mandan Historic Site and Lewis and Clark Interpretive Center

FORT MANDAN Nov. 2, 1804, to April 6, 1805

Bismarck

Claimed by the U.S. and Britain

St. Paul

Minneapolis

Mississippi River

Madison

Lake Oahe

Pierre

TENSE ENCOUNTER Lewis was under orders to foster good relations with the Teton Sioux, but through misunderstandings, the first meeting came close to violence several times

SEPARATE WAYS On the way east in 1806, Lewis rode on horseback to explore the Marias River, where he had a deadly encounter with Blackfeet. Clark traveled down the Yellowstone River by canoe

FAILED AMBUSHES Fearing encroachment on its territory, Spain sent four military missions to intercept and stop Lewis and Clark. None succeeded

Sioux City

Sergeant Floyd Monument

CASUALTY On Aug. 20, 1804, Sergeant Charles Floyd died, probably of an infected appendix. He was buried on a bluff in what is now Sioux City, Iowa

Omaha

Platte River

Lincoln

LOUISIANA PURCHASE

Became Louisiana Territory in 1805

Cheyenne

1st attempt ends

4th attempt ends

Topeka

Missouri River

Jefferson City

Kansas City

Denver

Claimed by the U.S. and Spain

5 **APRIL-AUGUST 1805**

INTO THE UNKNOWN

Lewis called the northern plains "beautifull in the extreme," but knew that harder times lay ahead. On May 26, he saw the Rockies for the first time. The Indians also had told of a large waterfall on the Missouri. Lewis reached the Great Falls on June 13, only to discover five falls over a 12-mile stretch

2nd attempt ends

Stopping point of 3rd Spanish attempt unknown

4 **WINTER 1804-05**

MANDAN VILLAGES

The corps spent the bitterly cold winter camped among thousands of Indians, along with French and British traders. A turning point of the expedition occurred when the captains signed on a French Canadian interpreter, who would bring along his young Shoshone wife Sacagawea

3 **MAY-NOVEMBER 1804**

UP THE MISSOURI

The river from St. Louis to the Mandan villages in what is now North Dakota was well traveled by trappers and traders, but the captains collected a trove of new plant and animal specimens and mapped the route carefully. Military discipline was strictly enforced, including the holding of courts-martial for desertion, drunkenness and sleeping on duty

Albuquerque

Santa Fe

Lewis carried an air rifle manufactured by Isaiah Lukens in Philadelphia. It had a compressed air reservoir in the stock and could fire 40 rounds before reloading

MAP AND TEXT BY JACKSON DYKMAN

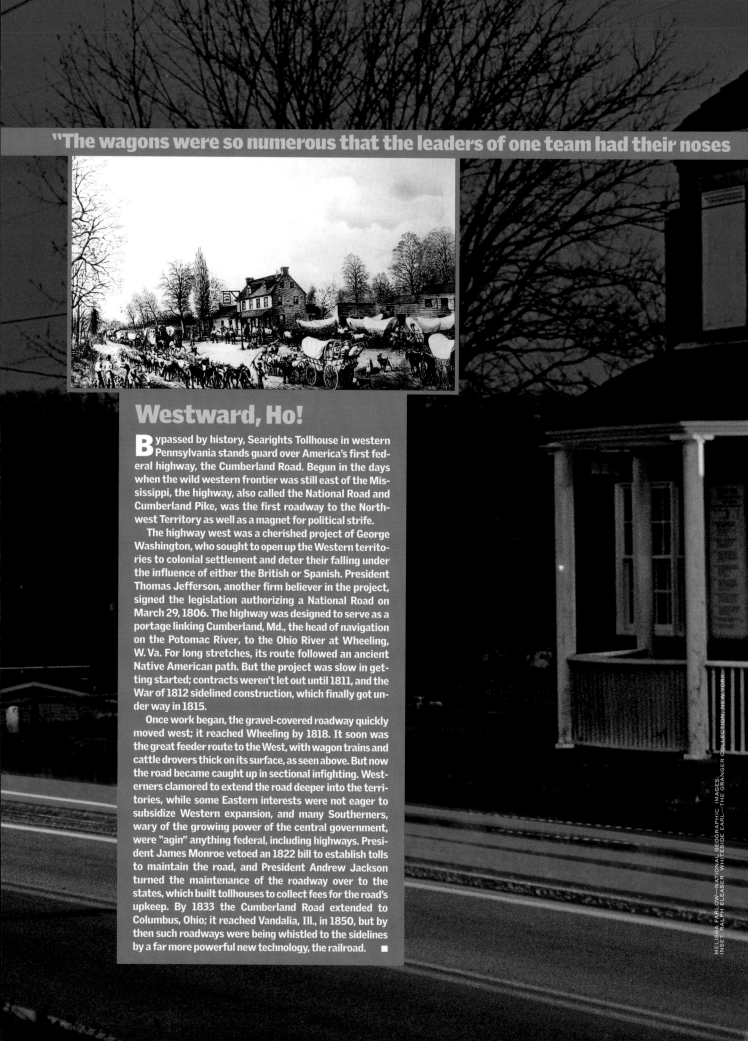

Westward, Ho!

Bypassed by history, Searights Tollhouse in western Pennsylvania stands guard over America's first federal highway, the Cumberland Road. Begun in the days when the wild western frontier was still east of the Mississippi, the highway, also called the National Road and Cumberland Pike, was the first roadway to the Northwest Territory as well as a magnet for political strife.

The highway west was a cherished project of George Washington, who sought to open up the Western territories to colonial settlement and deter their falling under the influence of either the British or Spanish. President Thomas Jefferson, another firm believer in the project, signed the legislation authorizing a National Road on March 29, 1806. The highway was designed to serve as a portage linking Cumberland, Md., the head of navigation on the Potomac River, to the Ohio River at Wheeling, W. Va. For long stretches, its route followed an ancient Native American path. But the project was slow in getting started; contracts weren't let out until 1811, and the War of 1812 sidelined construction, which finally got under way in 1815.

Once work began, the gravel-covered roadway quickly moved west; it reached Wheeling by 1818. It soon was the great feeder route to the West, with wagon trains and cattle drovers thick on its surface, as seen above. But now the road became caught up in sectional infighting. Westerners clamored to extend the road deeper into the territories, while some Eastern interests were not eager to subsidize Western expansion, and many Southerners, wary of the growing power of the central government, were "agin" anything federal, including highways. President James Monroe vetoed an 1822 bill to establish tolls to maintain the road, and President Andrew Jackson turned the maintenance of the roadway over to the states, which built tollhouses to collect fees for the road's upkeep. By 1833 the Cumberland Road extended to Columbus, Ohio; it reached Vandalia, Ill., in 1850, but by then such roadways were being whistled to the sidelines by a far more powerful new technology, the railroad. ∎

Cumberland Road

in the trough at the end of the next wagon ahead." —*Harper's* magazine, 1879

Wars in the Wilderness

As Indians and white settlers battle in the Northwest Territory, Tecumseh's confederation is beaten at the **Battle of Tippecanoe**

"Our Singers had warned us that a pale people would come across the Great

Inspired by the seer Tenskwatawa ("He Who Opens Doors"), Indians attack U.S. troops at Tippecanoe in today's Indiana; the Native Americans lost the battle

© IN 1889 BY KURZ & ALLISON, ART PUBLISHERS, CHICAGO, USA

IN THE YEARS AFTER THE REVOLUTIONary War, a steady stream of white settlers continued clearing the forests and building cabins in the Northwest Territory lands inhabited by Native Americans. Imperiled and outnumbered, tribes that had once been rivals reacted just as the colonies had done when facing the British: they united in common cause, carrying out a long-running, low-grade battle against the whites. In the early 1790s, President George Washington dispatched two expeditions to subdue the Indians, but both failed.

In 1792 Washington sent his old colleague from the Revolutionary War, General Anthony (Mad Anthony) Wayne to put down a rising coalition of Indian tribes led by the Miami chief, Little Turtle. After two years of skirmishing, the two sides finally met on Aug. 20, 1794, in a major engagement, the Battle of Fallen Timbers (named for the destruction of the forest by a recent tornado), on land outside today's Toledo. Wayne's troops thoroughly beat the Indians, now led by a Shawnee warrior, Blue Jacket, and in 1795 the Indians signed the Treaty of Greenville, deeding huge tracts of land to the U.S.

After several years of relative peace, a new Indian confederation arose in 1808, led by the Shawnee chief Tecumseh and his brother Tenskwatawa, a holy man and seer known as the Prophet. The two established a utopian community, Prophet's Town, near today's Lafayette, Ind., where they preached tribal unity and resistance to the whites. The young Governor of the Indiana Territory, William Henry Harrison, led an army of some 1,100 men against the Indians in the fall of 1811, while Tecumseh was in the southeastern territories, spreading his gospel of resistance to the Creek tribe. When Harrison's army drew near, the Prophet rallied the braves, promising them the white man's bullets could not harm them. He was mistaken. In the Battle of Tippecanoe, on Nov. 7, 1811, the Indians took the offensive and attacked the whites at dawn; they were beaten, barely, and Prophet's Town was burned.

Two years later, Tecumseh and his followers fought alongside their British allies in the War of 1812, but they were defeated by a U.S. army again led by Harrison, at the Battle of the Thames River in Ontario, and Tecumseh was killed. With his death, major Indian resistance to white settlement in the Northwest Territory also expired. ■

Water and try to destroy us, but we forgot." —Tenskwatawa

Territories to States, 1791-1821

Once America's freedom had been won, and the borders of the new nation had been firmly penciled in by the Treaty of 1783, the United States extended from the Atlantic Coast to the shores of the Mississippi. Now a difficult decision loomed: How should these vast territories be settled and governed? Long before, when the British Crown first handed out the land grants that became the colonies, American geography was so little known that the grants were generally extended infinitely to the west; as the terrain became better known, individual colonies claimed vast horizontal slices of the continent, stretching all the way to the Mississippi, as shown in the large map at right, drawn up in 1783.

The result was confusion and contention over competing state land claims. These were not the eloquent debates of Independence Hall but rather actual shooting wars in which, for example, Pennsylvania homesteaders fired on Connecticut settlers who claimed the Wyoming Valley under their state's old charter. The future, like much of the land, was entirely uncharted: at one point, settlers in Vermont, when still part of New York State, threatened to secede from the Union and join Canada.

In a show of Revolutionary unity, the "landed" states had already begun yielding to the demands of the "landless" states in the 1780s, surrendering their extravagant claims—New York in 1781, Virginia (the Virginia Military District south of the Ohio River) in 1784, Massachusetts in 1785 and Connecticut (the Western Reserve in northern Ohio) in 1785. Then the much maligned Congress of the Confederation stepped in with a solution: the Northwest Ordinance of 1787, passed even as the Constitutional Congress was meeting in hopes of making the Confederation obsolete. This farsighted plan called for the Northwest Territory—the lands north of the Ohio River, more than 260,000 sq. mi.—to be carved into no more than five states, which would be admitted to the Union as full equals with the original 13. They would be administered by a Governor, a secretary and three judges named by Congress. As soon as there were 5,000 free adult males in the territory, authority would reside in an elected legislature; when the population reached 60,000, the section would become a state.

Significantly, the Ordinance declared these new states would be free states, not slave states. Here was a great compromise: Southern states agreed to the plan because it tacitly endorsed the admission of an equal number of slave states from the Southeast—the new states entered in lockstep, one free, then one slave. In short, the Ordinance provided for an America whose house was divided, but whose citizens still lived under one roof.

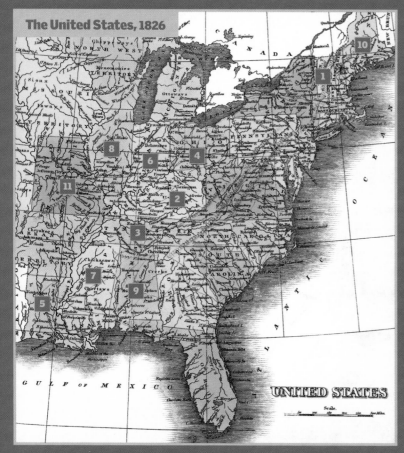

The United States, 1826

GULF OF MEXICO

UNITED STATES

Scale.

1. Vermont Admitted: 1791 (14). The Green Mountain State was home to Ethan Allen and his fellow militiamen, who captured Fort Ticonderoga in 1775. The first three states admitted to the Union were carefully chosen to balance free and slave states: Vermont, a free state broken off from New York, when matched with slave states Kentucky and Tennessee, made a Union of eight free and eight slave states.

2. Kentucky Admitted: 1792 (15). The first region west of the Alleghenies to be settled by American pioneers, Kentucky takes its name from the Iroquois word *Ken-tah-ten,* or "Land of Tomorrow." Daniel Boone led its settlement, opening the Cumberland Gap in 1775 via what is now known as the Wilderness Trail.

3. Tennessee Admitted: 1796 (16). First explored by Spaniard Hernando de Soto, this mountainous region was claimed by both France and Spain. In 1784-87, white settlers formed the "free state of Franklin" here; it later sent representatives to the North Carolina legislature.

4. Ohio Admitted: 1803 (17). The first permanent settlement here was established in 1788 at Marietta, capital of the Northwest Territory. General Anthony Wayne's victory over an Indian confederation in the Battle of Fallen Timbers (1794) paved the way for burgeoning white homesteading in this land named from an Iroquois word meaning "Great River."

5. Louisiana Admitted: 1812 (18). America's only state to still retain a strong French heritage, Louisiana—named for King Louis XIV—was admitted to the Union just as tense relations between Britain and the U.S. flared into war, ensuring U.S. control of the mouth of the Mississippi.

6. Indiana Admitted: 1816 (19). George Rogers Clark won major victories against the British here during the Revolutionary War, and when Territorial Governor William Henry Harrison defeated Tecumseh's coalition at Tippecanoe in 1811, white homesteading accelerated.

7. Mississippi Admitted: 1817 (20). Although Britain ceded its claim to the region in 1783, Spain retained its claim until 1798; in 1810 the U.S. annexed West Florida from Spain, including parts of southern Mississippi, affording the territory access to the Gulf of Mexico. Here King Cotton would reign through much of the 19th century.

8. Illinois Admitted: 1818 (21). French settlers established the first European settlement at Cahokia (near East St. Louis) in 1699; George Rogers Clark captured the fort here, by then in English hands, in 1778 for the colonies. Located along the Mississippi and the Great Lakes, the state became a great center of trade and industry.

9. Alabama Admitted: 1819 (22). First explored by the Spanish, the area was later settled by the French at Fort Louis de Mobile in 1702. Landlocked inside the Mississippi Territory by the Treaty of 1783, Alabama regained access to the Gulf of Mexico with the annexation of West Florida from Spain in 1810.

10. Maine Admitted: 1820 (23). The Pine Tree State, originally explored by English seafarers John and Sebastian Cabot, was long administered by Massachusetts. It entered the Union hand in hand with unlikely partner Missouri under the critical Missouri Compromise of 1820.

11. Missouri Admitted: 1821 (24). Visited by Hernando de Soto and later by French explorers of the Mississippi River, the region was first settled by French fur traders in 1735 at Ste. Genevieve, south of St. Louis (settled in 1764). The state is named for the Missouri Indian tribe; the term means "Town of the Large Canoes."

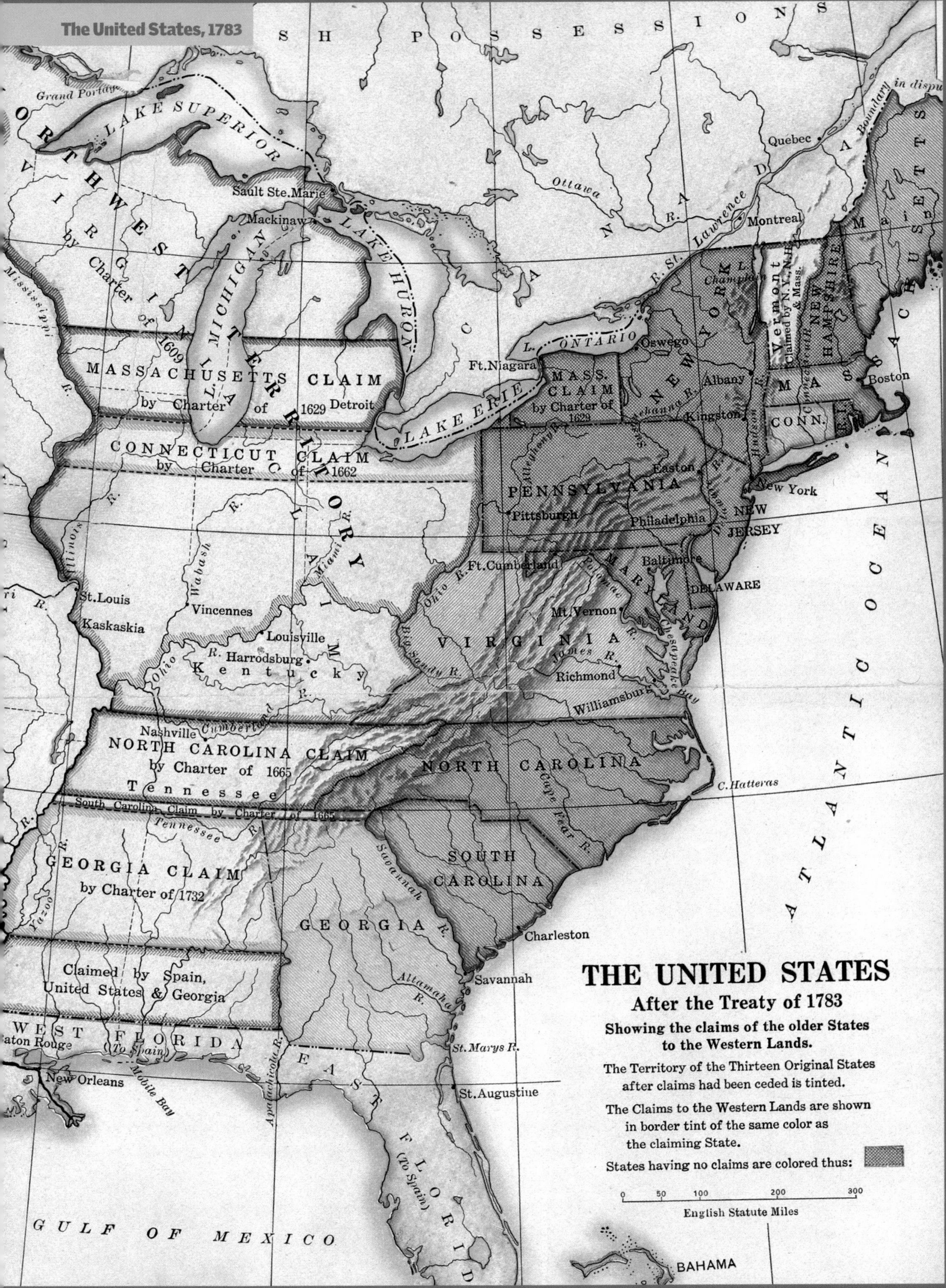

SH POSSESSIONS

NORTHWEST

Grand Portage

LAKE SUPERIOR

VIRGINIA by Charter of 1609

Sault Ste. Marie

Mackinaw

LAKE HURON

MICHIGAN

MASSACHUSETTS CLAIM by Charter of 1629

Detroit

CONNECTICUT CLAIM by Charter of 1662

Mississippi R.

Illinois R.

Wabash R.

St. Louis

Vincennes

Kaskaskia

Louisville

R. Harrodsburg

Kentucky

Nashville

Cumberland R.

NORTH CAROLINA CLAIM by Charter of 1665

Tennessee

South Carolina Claim by Charter of 1665

Tennessee R.

GEORGIA CLAIM by Charter of 1732

Yazoo R.

Claimed by Spain, United States & Georgia

WEST FLORIDA (To Spain)

Baton Rouge

New Orleans

Mobile Bay

GULF OF MEXICO

EAST FLORIDA (To Spain)

Apalachicola R.

Savannah R.

Altamaha R.

GEORGIA

Charleston

Savannah

St. Marys R.

St. Augustine

SOUTH CAROLINA

C. Fear R.

NORTH CAROLINA

C. Hatteras

Williamsburg

Richmond

VIRGINIA

Big Sandy R.

James R.

Mt. Vernon

Ft. Cumberland

MARYLAND

Baltimore

DELAWARE

Chesapeake Bay

PENNSYLVANIA

Pittsburgh

Philadelphia

NEW JERSEY

New York

Easton

MASS. CLAIM by Charter of 1629

Ft. Niagara

LAKE ERIE

L. ONTARIO

Oswego

Albany

Kingston

CONN.

NEW YORK

Hudson R.

Vermont Claimed by N.Y., N.H. & Mass.

NEW HAMPSHIRE

MASSACHUSETTS

Boston

Maine

L. Champlain

R. St. Lawrence

Montreal

Quebec

Boundary in dispute

CANADA

Ottawa R.

ATLANTIC OCEAN

BAHAMA

THE UNITED STATES
After the Treaty of 1783
Showing the claims of the older States to the Western Lands.

The Territory of the Thirteen Original States after claims had been ceded is tinted.

The Claims to the Western Lands are shown in border tint of the same color as the claiming State.

States having no claims are colored thus:

0   50   100   200   300

English Statute Miles

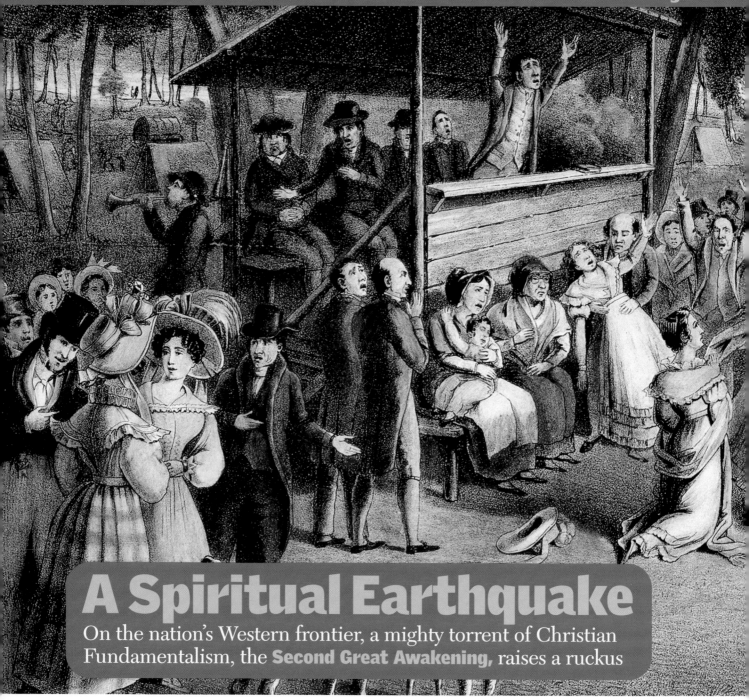

A Spiritual Earthquake

On the nation's Western frontier, a mighty torrent of Christian Fundamentalism, the **Second Great Awakening,** raises a ruckus

BILLY GRAHAM WOULD HAVE KNOWN JUST WHAT TO DO IF he had found himself at Cane Ridge, Ky., in August 1801: like the wandering preachers around him, he would have jumped onto a wagon or stage and begun making a joyful noise unto the Lord, promising sinners redemption and salvation through a personal encounter with Jesus Christ, mankind's savior. For the Rev. Graham's ministry—like that of Joel Osteen, Jerry Falwell and other Christian evangelists of our day—still draws on the deep well of Christian revival practices whose waters were first tapped in the mighty religious upsurge of the early 19th century, the Second Great Awakening.

Just as the nation's political energies shifted westward as wilderness clearings grew into lively towns, these new religious impulses didn't look back to the Calvinist churches of Massachusetts or the Episcopal cathedrals of Virginia for inspiration: no, this raucous, energetic form of Christianity bore the rawboned stamp of its frontier origins. A wild and woolly, hooting and hollering form of religion, it emphasized the personal experience of a spiritual rebirth in which the soul was cleansed, restored anew by baptism, then enlisted in the mission of spreading, or evangelizing, the good news of the Gospel.

The preachers who led the revival called it the Second

This view of a camp meeting dates from 1830, three decades after the Second Great Awakening began, but its practices would be familiar to the settlers who thronged the campsite at Cane Ridge, Ky., in 1801

Great Awakening, in homage to the upsurge of religious enthusiasm that had rocked the colonies in the early 1700s, led by such preachers as Jonathan Edwards. The hallmark and drawing card of the movement was a new invention, the camp meeting, in which settlers from many miles around converged on a large campground to hear a variety of preachers hold forth. That such get-togethers allowed lonely frontier folk an opportunity to socialize, trade and barter goods, talk politics and pitch a little woo no doubt played a large role in their enormous popularity—but why tell the preacher that?

The defining moment of the new evangelism was the 1801 gathering at Cane Ridge, where as many as 25,000 people came together, at a time when Kentucky's largest city, Lexington, had a population of 1,795. Filled with the sounds of hymns and the cries of weeping, saved sinners, this joyful, muscular new Christianity pushed aside the predestination and gloom of the old Calvinists, while it moved the emphasis away from one's formal denomination to one's personal experience of Christ. Like today's Fundamentalists, it preached a Second Coming in which the righteous would prevail and sinners would wail. Two centuries later, that first frontier revival remains the seminal wake-up call of American evangelism. ■

Rembrandt of a New Eden

A young Frenchman, **John James Audubon,** transforms himself into "the American Woodsman" and finds a wilderness ready for its close-up

MAIN IMAGE: NATIONAL HISTORICAL SOCIETY. INSET: THE WHITE HOUSE

IN THE YEAR 1803, RESIDENTS of Pennsylvania some 24 miles north of Philadelphia often came upon an unusual figure in the woods: a tall, muscular 18-year-old who wandered the deep forests of the region sketching birds from life while clad in the satin knee breeches of a well-to-do Frenchman, which he was. The young man, John James Audubon, was the illegitimate child of a wealthy French ship owner and planter and his chambermaid. Born on his father's plantation in Santo Domingo in 1785, Audubon was raised in Nantes, France, by his father and an understanding stepmother. He was given the education expected of a French aristocrat, with an emphasis on the fine arts, and he is said to have displayed his talent for drawing at an early age.

Audubon was a new arrival: he had sailed from France to America in order to avoid conscription into Napoleon's armies, taking up residence at his father's rural estate, Mill Grove, a 284-acre farm on Perkiomen Creek, a tributary of the Schuylkill River, where he lived in a stone farmhouse built in 1762. He soon was enchanted, besotted, with the American wilderness. Gradually shedding his formal clothing for simpler garb, he became a complete outdoorsman who hunted, collected, stuffed and sketched specimens of the wondrous menagerie he found all around him. A dedicated natural scientist, he was the first person in America to study the habits of birds by placing bands around their legs, determining from his research that the Eastern phoebes on his estate migrated south and returned north to the same nests every year.

After three years in America, Audubon went back to France; he returned to the U.S. in 1806 with two goals in mind: to marry the vibrant young Englishwoman, Lucy Bakewell, who was his neighbor at Mill Grove (she said yes)—and to create a painted archive of every species of bird in America "in its natural size and colouring."

It was an ambition equal to the landscape that inspired it, and it echoes Ralph Waldo Emerson's famous charge against Walt Whitman. The great poet, Emerson claimed, "set out to sing the songs of America, but seemed content to take its inventory." Audubon was more than content to take the inven-

"In Pennsylvania, a beautiful state ... I commenced my simple ... studies,

Above, a roseate spoonbill *(Ajaia ajaja)*. The portrait at upper left, painted in 1826 by John Syme, glorifies Audubon as a child of the frontier

with as little concern about the future as if the world had been made for me."

Reddish egrets (*Egretta Rufescens*)

tory of the great American aviary and fix it on canvas, and the project consumed his adult life. Eager to see and paint every habitat in this new Eden, he set out for the western frontier after his family fortune petered out, moving to Kentucky and opening a dry-goods store in Henderson. But he was a poor businessman, preferring to wander the woods with his rifle and sketchbook in hand, and after his store failed in 1819, he devoted himself to his grand obsession.

For the next four years Audubon wandered through the South, eking out a living doing odd jobs, while the steadfast Lucy raised his two sons, often amid privation. Growing in his craft, Audubon discovered that he could use wires to mount his dead specimens in natural attitudes, and this technical breakthrough gave his work a lively, sympathetic authenticity that still dazzles viewers. Watercolor was his chief medium, but he also employed other materials, mixing media—gouache, pastels, watercolor and glazes—on the same canvas.

When Audubon returned to the East Coast in 1824 with his portfolio, his bluster and self-promotion alienated the staid members of the Academy of Natural Sciences, who favored the earlier bird paintings of a local artist, Scotsman Alexander Wilson. Audubon sailed to England, where his work was an immediate success. Echoing Ben Franklin (and anticipating Buffalo Bill Cody), the painter styled himself "the American Woodsman" and promoted his frontier persona by wearing buckskins and dressing his hair with bear grease. When the first volume of his masterwork, *The Birds of America*, was published in 1827, it confirmed his genius. Printed in a huge double-elephant format, each 2-ft. by 3-ft. image was a window opening onto a marvelous American Arcadia. The work brought Audubon fame and security, and for the next two decades, until his death in 1851, he continued his travels, often assisted by his two sons, painting America's wildlife inventory in pellucid images that still carry the hushed expectancy of a nation at dawn—and an Eden at twilight. ■

American flamingo *(Phoenicopterus ruper)*

Common egret *(Casmerodius albus)*

Seeking Direction

Commodore Oliver Hazard Perry changes flagships at the Battle of Lake Erie

Growth Spurt: 1804-26

1804
Lewis and Clark Expedition sets out

1805
Thomas Jefferson begins second term as President

1809
James Madison, a Jefferson ally, becomes fourth President

1810
Anti-British War Hawks dominate congressional elections

1812
War of 1812 begins

1813
U.S. Navy wins Battle of Lake Erie

1814
British burn Washington; Frances Scott Key writes *The Star-Spangled Banner;* Treaty of Ghent technically ends War of 1812

1815
U.S. forces under Andrew Jackson defeat British at Battle of New Orleans

1817
James Monroe's election as fifth President begins "Era of Good Feelings"

1820
Missouri Compromise will admit Maine (free state) and Missouri (slave state) to Union

1823
Monroe Doctrine is issued, slowing European colonization of Americas

1824
John Quincy Adams is elected over Jackson in the "corrupt bargain" with Henry Clay, dividing nation

1825
Erie Canal opens

1826
John Adams and Thomas Jefferson die on July 4, the 50th anniversary of the approval of the Declaration of Independence

Simply Complex

WE ARE ALL FEDERALISTS," THOMAS JEFFERSON said in his 1801 Inaugural Address, "and we are all Republicans." If this attempt to heal the divisions underlying his bitterly contested victory over John Adams was understandable, it was also a striking statement, coming from a man who claimed to detest all political parties ("If I could not go to heaven but with a party," he once said, "I would not go there at all") yet who helped found the Democratic-Republicans. Jefferson had sought the presidency, despite being profoundly wary of its powers. Even before taking the oath of office, he made a gesture that would be mimicked by modern Presidents, from Jimmy Carter to George W. Bush: he refused the ornate carriage that had been reserved for him and walked to his Inauguration. Among his first acts in office was to drop the regal court etiquette that had been practiced by Washington and, to a lesser extent, by Adams.

Ironically, history conspired to make this reluctant President a more activist Chief Executive than either of his predecessors. When the Barbary pirates of northern Africa continued their raids on U.S. merchant ships, Jefferson abandoned the pay-for-peace policy of Washington and Adams (who had given the pirates almost $2 million in tribute and ransom), built up the U.S. Navy and sent it to deal with the thieves. When Napoleon pronounced himself ready to part with the vast territory of Louisiana, Jefferson (who abhorred large government expenditures) agreed to pay $15 million to double the size of the nation in a single stroke. That he had to issue government bonds to buy the land, and that the Constitution didn't specifically empower the President to expand the nation's borders, troubled Jefferson but didn't stop him. When Royal Navy ships, short of manpower during the Napoleonic Wars, began abducting American sailors at gunpoint on the high seas, Jefferson responded with the Embargo Act of 1807, which suspended U.S. trade with European nations and barred British ships from American waters, setting the stage for the War of 1812.

To the end of his life, Jefferson remained profoundly ambivalent about having held the reins of power. Before he died, he left instructions that the headstone above his grave should note his writing of the Declaration of Independence and his founding of the University of Virginia—but pilgrims visiting today see no mention of his presidency. ■

"I had rather be shut up ... with my books, my family and a few old friends ...

Gilbert Stuart painted this portrait of Jefferson circa 1805-07, in the second term of his presidency

President Thomas Jefferson

than to occupy the most splendid post, which any human power can give."

James Madison

"What is government itself, but the greatest of all reflections on human nature? If men were angels, no government would be necessary."

Eternal, Paternal Glory

LIKE MODERN PHYSICIST STEPHEN HAWKING, JAMES MADI-son was one of those geniuses whose life force seems channeled directly into the brain, bypassing the body. A small, sickly man, Madison had the look of a 60-year-old when he was still in his 40s; Washington Irving once described him as "but a withered little apple-John." What delicious revenge it must have been for the life-long bachelor to marry, at 43, a woman 17 years his junior whose style would become legendary, the widow Dolley Todd. The couple had no children, yet Madison's greatest achievement is indeed paternal—and, Americans hope, eternal. He is the Father of the Constitution.

Known from his youth for his sheer intellectual horsepower, Madison attracted the attention and friendship of Thomas Jefferson soon after his graduation from the College of New Jersey (later Princeton University). Too frail to serve in uniform during the Revolution, Madison was named a delegate to the Continental Congress, thanks to Jefferson's backing. Al-though his voice was quiet, it told; he soon impressed his fellow delegates with his scholarly approach to political issues.

After the war, Madison championed, with Alexander Hamilton, a new convention to address the weaknesses of the Articles of Confederation. He dominated the Constitutional Convention of 1787, early on presenting his Virginia Plan, whose tripartite structure of executive, legislative and judicial bodies, kept in tension by a system of checks and balances, has not only served America well but has also become a template for governments worldwide. With Hamilton and John Jay, Madison explored the nature of government and promoted the adoption of the Constitution in the great *Federalist* papers.

Jefferson's closest adviser, Madison followed his fellow Virginian into the White House in 1809, where he found his interests aligning with the bellicose War Hawks. In a final irony, this peaceful theorist of power led his nation into the War of 1812, which his enemies dubbed "Mr. Madison's War." ■

First of First Ladies

DOLLEY MADISON PLAYED THE ROLE OF FIRST Lady to perfection; after all, she invented it. She was raised a Quaker and taught to value simplicity, yet she became the greatest hostess and style setter of her time. Married in 1790 at 22 to Philadelphia lawyer John Todd, she was widowed three years later when a yellow fever epidemic claimed both her husband and their youngest son. Beautiful and buxom, witty and vivacious, Dolley Todd soon caught the eye of James Madison, the brilliant Virginia Congressman. Although he was 17 years older than she, the two married in 1794; three years later, Madison retired from politics and they moved to his family estate, Montpelier, in Virginia, intending to settle into a life as plantation grandees.

President Thomas Jefferson had other ideas; he asked Madison to be his Secretary of State, and in 1801 the couple moved to Washington. For the following 16 years, Dolley presided over White House functions; Jefferson was a widower, and the socially accomplished Mrs. Madison served for eight years as his unofficial First Lady. When her husband became President in 1809, Dolley turned the executive mansion into a glittering social center distinguished by an ease tailored to a democracy rather than a monarchy. Colorful, quotable and independent, Dolley dipped snuff and argued for women's rights while scandalizing some with her expensive dresses and turbans.

When the British burned the White House in 1814, Dolley personally saved the great Gilbert Stuart portrait of Washington—and one of herself. She and Madison moved back to Montpelier in 1817, but after his death in 1836, she returned to the capital; for the next 12 years she reigned again as the doyen of local society, revered as a last living link to the Founders. ■

Dolley Madison

"There is one secret, and that is the power we all have in forming our own destinies."

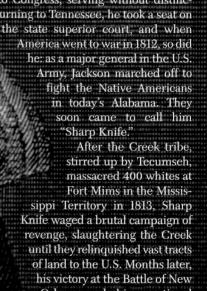

Young Hickory

ANDREW JACKSON WAS THE EMBODIMENT OF THE frontier. His election to the presidency in 1828 marked a mighty shift in national politics: the age of revolution, dominated by the refined men of the East, was over; a rugged age of Western expansion had begun. But it's not the "Old Hickory" of 1828 we're concerned with in this book: it's the young Jackson, a hot-tempered, rip-roaring, saloon-trashing upstart of very humble birth. This Jackson was orphaned at 14 and fought in the Revolution as a teenager. This Jackson earned a national reputation as a ruthless exterminator of Indians. This Jackson defended his honor in two or three duels and carried a bullet in his shoulder throughout his life, a relic of a shootout.

A native of the Carolinas, Jackson studied law in his 20s, then moved to Tennessee, where he became a lawyer, served as a judge and was elected to Congress, serving without distinction. Returning to Tennessee, he took a seat on the state superior court, and when America went to war in 1812, so did he: as a major general in the U.S. Army, Jackson marched off to fight the Native Americans in today's Alabama. They soon came to call him "Sharp Knife."

After the Creek tribe, stirred up by Tecumseh, massacred 400 whites at Fort Mims in the Mississippi Territory in 1813, Sharp Knife waged a brutal campaign of revenge, slaughtering the Creek until they relinquished vast tracts of land to the U.S. Months later, his victory at the Battle of New Orleans made him a national hero, perhaps America's closest equivalent to that classic European figure, "the man on horseback." ■

Andrew Jackson

"I am at the head of 2,070 volunteers ... who have no constitutional scruples"

Stellar Speller

AMERICA'S WASHINGTON OF WORDS, NOAH Webster, took the hand-me-down language of the colonies and drilled it into shape, creating a leaner, regularized version of English that declared its independence from Britain. Although Webster would reach his greatest fame in 1828, with the publication of his celebrated dictionary, he began influencing the way Americans spoke and wrote four decades earlier, in 1785, when he completed the publication of *A Grammatical Institute of the English Language*. The groundbreaking work was divided into three parts: a grammar, a reader and a speller. Three years later, Webster published a stand-alone, updated version of the speller, and it was this book that became a basic necessity in striving colonial households. Even Ben Franklin, who once said that he "had no use for a man with but one spelling for a word," embraced the slim volume that came to be known as "The Blue-Backed Speller." By some estimates, Webster published as many as 300 different editions of the book between 1788 and 1829.

Born in 1758 in Hartford, Conn., Webster was educated at Yale University and hoped to study law, but financial necessity drove him to teaching. Revulsed by the crowded classrooms and the lack of standardized texts he found, Webster took to lexicography. A true child of colonial New England, he was preachy, censorious and severe; writer Bill Bryson summed him up as "short, pale, smug and boastful." But whatever his personal flaws, Webster is the Founding Father of the American language, the man who regularized its spelling and pronunciation. The industrious Yankee helped pioneer copyright law in the U.S. and was a founder of Amherst College but was less successful in his other ventures: he started up various newspapers and magazines that failed, and in 1833 he published a heavily bowdlerized version of the Bible, in which a modest Onan "frustrates his purpose" rather than "spills his seed." It failed to find fertile ground among readers. ■

Noah Webster

"Language is not an abstract ... its bases [are] broad and low, close to the ground."

A Continent in Flames

Angry at the British, coveting Canada and frightened about its frontiers, a bellicose Congress launches the **War of 1812**

IF YOU HAVE ONLY A VAGUE IDEA OF WHAT THE WAR OF 1812 was about—Frances Scott Key wrote *The Star-Spangled Banner*, the British burned the White House, Andrew Jackson won the Battle of New Orleans, and "Old Ironsides" did something or another—don't be discouraged: you have about as clear a notion of the war's goals and progress as the statesmen who led it and the soldiers who fought it. Like the Korean War, sandwiched between the triumphs of World War II and the divisions of Vietnam, the War of 1812 sits orphaned between two American milestones: the glory of the Revolution and the tragedy of the Civil War. As with the Korean War too, the fortunes of both sides in the War of 1812 gyrated wildly from one campaign to the next, but the drama ended in stalemate, with neither side having gained much of anything. Yet even if no territory changed hands, the War of 1812 changed minds. Americans came to see themselves as masters of their destiny. And the rest of the world came to view this upstart Union of former colonies as a full-fledged member of the community of nations.

In the first decade of the 19th century, American statesmen faced two dilemmas, one internal and one international. At home, the country's growing population and humming economy clamored for expansion. But in every direction, the young nation was hemmed in: Native American tribes held the land to the west, while European powers claimed all the territory to the north and south. Canada remained a British possession, while Spain still held the territory that would become Alabama and Florida. Abroad, U.S. leaders had been trying for more than a decade to steer a middle course between France and Britain, which had been at war since 1793. Washington's policy consisted of neutrality and a willingness to trade with both sides. But when the fighting in Europe intensified in 1803, each European power put renewed pressure on the United States to stop selling food and other vital raw materials to its enemy.

Americans resented such pressure from either side, but the British were far more heavy-handed than the French in its application. Royal Navy ships routinely fired upon and boarded American vessels crossing the Atlantic. If an American ship was bound for France, the boat and its cargo would often be seized and sold. Even more galling, the British, who were desperately short of manpower, would frequently search any American ship, regardless of its destination, under the pretext of looking for British deserters and take away in chains however many sailors the captain needed.

This "impressment" of as many as 10,000 U.S. citizens into British service at the point of a gun was the single most inflammatory issue exploited by the American leaders who now began arguing for war. A close second was the widely held

As the White House burns, citizens attempt to douse the fires set by the British in this undated, imaginative scene

"Ay, tear her tattered ensign down!/ Long has it waved on high/ And many an

American belief, which had considerable basis in fact, that the British were arming and instigating the Western tribes of Native Americans in their violent resistance to white expansion beyond the Ohio River. By 1810, this resistance had flared into open warfare. A confederation of several Indian tribes, led by the Shawnee chief Tecumseh, were using British arms to halt the westward movement of U.S. traders and settlers. Tecumseh also journeyed south and enlisted the Creek tribe, native to Georgia, Alabama and Florida, to join his confederation. Soon the Creek were staging military raids against whites in the Southeastern United States.

Amid this discord, the election of 1810 was a landmark: more than half the seats in the House of Representatives turned over, as Americans voted to resolve their problems with the British and Tecumseh. A group of self-proclaimed War Hawks now dominated the House. Led by Henry Clay of Kentucky and John C. Calhoun of South Carolina, they quickly passed Macon's Bill No. 2, proposed by North Carolina's Nathaniel Macon, which threatened a complete embargo of all U.S. trade against any European power that continued to seize American ships. The French quickly complied. But the British defied the act—as Clay and Calhoun had hoped—bringing the two nations one step closer to war. The War Hawks' position was further strengthened in 1811, when U.S. soldiers under General William Henry Harrison scored a decisive victory over Tecumseh at the Battle of Tippecanoe, in present-day Indiana.

The following year, President James Madison faced a difficult campaign for re-election. He had been resisting the calls for war since 1810; now, eager to shore up his support in the South and West, he began to side with the War Hawks. At the same time, British naval vessels began blockading most American ports, an act tantamount to war. On June 1, 1812, Madison sent a message to Congress enumerating America's

grievances against England and asking that war be declared between the United States and Britain. Three days later, the motion easily passed the House of Representatives, the abode of the War Hawks.

The Senate debated the measure for two more weeks. During this time, Britain announced it would comply with Macon's bill and lift the coastal blockade, cease the impressment of American sailors and stop seizing U.S. ships. Fully engaged with the struggle against Napoleon, the British were not eager to wage a war in North America. If the telegraph had been available in 1812, news of London's concessions would have arrived in Washington in time to prevent war. As it was, word came by ship and did not arrive for several weeks. And by then, the U.S. Senate had passed Madison's resolution, and America's first formally declared war had begun.

BOTH SIDES WERE COMPLETELY UNPREPARED FOR WAR. The British, taxed to the limits of their resources by the Napoleonic Wars, had fewer than 10,000 men on Canadian soil and aboard British ships in the Atlantic. The addition of Canadian militia and Native American allies brought their total troop strength to just over 100,000. The American side had a poorly trained and ill-equipped army of approximately 60,000 men. State militias would bring American troop strength up to around 500,000 men—most of whom were unwilling to fight outside the borders of their own states.

Canada was Britain's last outpost in North America, and a restless, if generally unstated, hope activated the War Hawks who had plunged America into war: the vast lands to the north might form future states for the U.S. Tens of thousands of American Loyalists had fled to Canada during the war, and devotion to the Crown ran high in the north; as in the Revolutionary War, Canada's future was in play in this new conflict. Thomas Jefferson predicted that conquering Canada would be merely "a matter of marching." He was decidedly wrong.

Less than a month after the declaration of war, U.S. General William Hull invaded Canada from Detroit. In four weeks of combat, British General Isaac Brock repelled the invasion, then tricked Hull into surrendering his Detroit garrison to a numerically inferior force of guerrillas from Tecumseh's federation. So disgraceful (and so unexpected) was this defeat that Hull was court-martialed and sentenced to be shot. He was pardoned and allowed to retire only after the personal intervention of President Madison.

Now in possession of Detroit (and much of Michigan), Brock raced to the eastern end of Lake Erie, where he met a second invasion force, led by American General Henry Dearborn. A respected veteran of the Revolution who had served at Lexington and Concord, Dearborn was an ineffective commander whose refusal to coordinate his actions with Hull was one of the principal reasons for the loss of Detroit and symptomatic of a problem that plagued the Americans throughout the war: their generals often viewed one another as rivals, at best, and more often as adversaries.

At the Battle of Queenston Heights on Oct. 13, 1812, an American force of more than 6,000 men crossed the Niagara River to confront Brock's contingent of fewer than 300 troops,

navy was committed to the western Atlantic, but that tiny contingent still dwarfed America's entire fleet: 11 major battleships, 34 frigates and more than 40 smaller gunboats.

Yet numbers don't tell the whole story. The Royal Navy's armada in America had a staggering roster of duties: escorting British merchant ships through tens of thousands of square miles of unfriendly waters, blockading the entire East Coast of the U.S. and hunting down U.S. Navy warships. By contrast, the much smaller American force had only to stalk English trading vessels whenever they could be found unescorted, ambush Royal Navy ships when they could be caught by surprise or in inferior numbers and hide the rest of the time.

The U.S. Navy soon found action. In August the U.S.S. *Constitution* met the British frigate H.M.S. *Guerrière* off the coast of Nova Scotia. In a 20-minute battle, the *Guerrière's* mainmast was shot down, the British commander surrendered, and Captain Isaac Hull (nephew and adopted son of the Army general who had been humiliated weeks earlier at Detroit) burned the captured vessel down to the waterline. By the end of the year, the *Constitution* was ranging as far south as Brazil, where she came upon the British frigate H.M.S. *Java*. After a three-hour engagement, the *Java* was also reduced to ashes.

In these engagements the British were finally paying the

eye has danced to see/ That banner in the sky." —Oliver Wendell Holmes

which was reinforced to a strength of 1,000 over the next few hours. But superior numbers were no match for superior organization and training. The British savaged the Americans as they crossed, then trapped and shredded the units that made it to their side of the river. When the smoke cleared, more than 500 Americans had been killed or wounded and another 1,000 taken prisoner. Only 14 British soldiers were dead and fewer than 100 wounded. The only good news for the Americans was that Brock, whose dashing leadership was indispensable to the British, was among the English dead.

With the onset of cold weather, both armies settled into winter quarters. The one ghastly exception to the pause in the shooting came in January 1813. President Madison had appointed General Harrison, the hero of Tippecanoe, to lead an expedition of Kentucky militiamen aimed at recapturing Detroit. As a detachment of these forces bivouacked beside the Raisin River, about 20 miles south of Detroit, they were surrounded and outnumbered by British troops and their Native American allies from the Wyandot tribe. After a brief skirmish on Jan. 22, the Americans surrendered and the British commander left the Indians in charge of his 60 colonial prisoners. The Wyandot chief, Roundhead, ordered them all killed. This massacre, and the rallying cry "Remember the Raisin!" would galvanize U.S. troops and American public opinion for the rest of the war.

WHILE AMERICA'S ARMY STUMBLED, ITS INfant Navy, from which neither side had expected much, distinguished itself beyond all expectation. In 1812 America's Navy consisted of only 20 vessels: six medium-sized frigates and 14 smaller vessels. Only a sliver of Britain's vast

Artifact

The liveliest artifact featured in this book is the venerable U.S. Navy frigate U.S.S. *Constitution,* visited yearly by tourists from around the world at its berth in the Charlestown Navy Yard. The ship was built in 1797 and carried 44 cannons and a crew of 450. It saw duty in the undeclared naval war with France in 1798-1800, sailed to North Africa to take on the Barbary pirates in the early 1800s, then scored memorable victories over H.M.S. *Guerrière* and H.M.S. *Java* in the War of 1812. The ship was scheduled to be scrapped in 1830, inspiring Oliver Wendell Holmes' poem that christened it "Old Ironsides"—and led to public donations that preserved it. Reconstructed in 1925, the ship takes an annual cruise, below, in which it is towed into the harbor and turned around, ensuring that both its sides are exposed equally to wind and weather.

price for years of impressment: many of the crew on British ships were serving against their will, while the U.S. vessels were manned by volunteers. The difference in motivation and morale contributed to a string of American victories against bigger ships with heavier and more numerous guns.

DURING THE COLD-WEATHER LULL IN THE LAND WAR, BOTH sides realized that control of the Great Lakes and the St. Lawrence River might determine Canada's fate. On the northwestern front, both sides spent the winter building ships a thousand miles from the nearest ocean.

By April 1813, American forces were ready to invade Canada for the third time. Ferried across Lake Ontario by the new fleet, American troops under General Dearborn were supposed to attack the British naval station at Kingston, then move on to the colonial capital city of York, now Toronto. This would have given the Americans uncontested control of Lake Ontario and possession of the eastern end of the St. Lawrence River, putting Montreal and Quebec within reach.

But Dearborn ignored his orders, bypassing Kingston and attacking York first. The Americans took the lightly defended capital almost without opposition, then burned the city to the ground, an insult the British would soon repay in kind. During the chaos that ensued, a British munitions depot exploded, killing hundreds of troops from both sides. After a few weeks of holding the devastated capital, the Americans realized it had little value without Kingston and abandoned it. Dearborn did manage one achievement; his troops plundered guns and ammunition from British stockpiles at York that would be badly needed in a lake battle several months later.

Throughout the war, American troops had whatever supplies they needed close at hand. But the supply line for Britain's troops in Canada stretched across the Atlantic Ocean, traveled the length of the St. Lawrence River, then spanned the breadth of the Great Lakes. Before supplies could reach the remote English garrison on the western end of Lake Erie, they had to pass through every British position along this 3,700-mile chain. And each of these outposts, itself hungry for supplies, would keep some of the shipment. This trickle of

supplies was choked off even further by U.S. raids across lakes Ontario and Erie.

By the late summer of 1813, the British outpost at Detroit was in near desperate condition. Soldiers and sailors had been living on half-rations for months. Weapons were in disrepair, and ammunition stocks were dangerously low. Even so, the British had managed during the previous winter to build a fleet of six new gunboats, including the flagship H.M.S. *Detroit*. Realizing that time was working against him, the English naval commander, Robert Barclay, decided to use his fleet to break out of the Detroit garrison and restore the flow of supplies across Lake Erie.

On Sept. 10, 1813, Barclay's fleet ran into the armada of nine vessels the Americans had built during the winter, now fitted with the British artillery captured by Dearborn. Commanded by Oliver Hazard Perry, the Americans set upon the British squadron near Put-in-Bay, Ohio. In a furious, four-hour gun battle, the ships fired upon each other from point-blank range. When Perry's flagship, the U.S.S. *Lawrence*, foundered, he rowed half a mile through heavy fire to transfer his command to the U.S.S. *Niagara*. So intense was the fighting that only 20 men from the *Lawrence's* crew of more than 100 escaped death or serious injury.

Realizing that his short-range guns were useless against the British unless he drew close, Perry boldly ordered the *Niagara* to drive straight through the British line. By this time, Barclay had been wounded and was belowdecks being treated. Perry's unexpected maneuver confused the less-experienced officers he had left in command, and British attempts to reposition their ships quickly turned into a bloody fiasco. For the first time in its history, the Royal Navy lost not only an en-

On May 4, 1814, a British invasion force captured Fort Oswego, N.Y., on Lake Ontario. This painting is based on a sketch made by Lieut. John Hewitt of the Royal Marines, a hero of the battle

gagement but also an entire fleet: every vessel that Barclay had sent into battle was captured or destroyed. Shortly afterward, Perry sat down to write a report of the battle and penned the immortal words, "We have met the enemy and they are ours."

The White House in ruins in August 1814 following the British occupation and arson

THE BATTLE OF LAKE ERIE GAVE THE AMERICANS FRESH energy. General Harrison, stalled by the winter almost a year earlier, now mounted the fourth American incursion into Canada. After Barclay's defeat on the water, English General Henry Proctor had abandoned British positions all around Lake Erie and retreated farther into Canada, along with Tecumseh and his legions of Native American warriors. Harrison chased them to the shores of the Thames River, near Chatham, Ont. When the British and their tribal confederates turned to fight, Harrison abandoned what had been American tactical orthodoxy since the Revolution and charged directly into the British line. Panicked, the English troops broke ranks and fled.

Tecumseh, however, was not made for flight. In a display of courage that would cost him and his warriors their lives, the braves stood fast in the face of the American onslaught. When the Shawnee chief fell, the British lost more than a staunch ally: his death marked the end of the alliance among Indian nations that Tecumseh had forged. Harrison later paid tribute to his adversary by calling him "one of those uncommon geniuses which spring up occasionally to produce revolutions and overturn the established order of things."

Lake Erie and the Canadian territory surrounding it were now firmly in American control and would remain so for the rest of the war. The obvious next step was to attack British positions on Lake Ontario. But once again, rivalries within the chain of command stood in the way of victory. Two American generals, Wade Hampton and James Wilkinson, were chosen to lead simultaneous attacks on the British stronghold at Montreal from different directions. But Hampton and Wilkinson detested each other; both retreated after minor skirmishes, and Montreal, though vulnerable, was left unscathed.

In the north, the spring of 1814 brought another botched American attempt to wrest control of Lake Ontario from the British. This led to the bloodiest engagement of the war, the Battle of Lundy's Lane, north of Niagara Falls, in which a large U.S. column stumbled into the sights of a massive British artillery emplacement, suffering the loss of some 1,800 men in only five hours.

Realizing that in the wake of Napoleon's April 1814 abdication, the British were now able to bring fresh resources to the war with the U.S., Washington scaled back its ambitions. This would be the last attempt to invade Canada. In September, the British invaded the United States from Canada, but a similar lack of coordination led to their defeat on Lake Champlain at the Battle of Plattsburgh.

Seizing the initiative, the British decided to take the war to America's capital, reinforcing their Atlantic coastal blockade and venturing into Chesapeake Bay. By August, they were far enough up the Potomac River to threaten Washington and Baltimore. On Aug. 24 British troops came ashore in Maryland and, although heavily outnumbered, whipped a small, inexperienced detachment of local militia that met them at Bladensberg, then marched unopposed toward the capital.

A surprised James Madison and his wife Dolley had to flee the White House on such short notice that British commanders were able to sit down to a meal that had been prepared for them. After dining, they took revenge for the destruction of York a year earlier, setting every public building in Washington aflame. The White House, made up mostly of wood and plaster, burned easily. The Capitol, built from stone, was more difficult to destroy, but the British made a point of starting separate fires in each of its several hundred rooms, placing bales of kindling on the wooden floors and window frames.

After a few days of these diversions, the British marched toward their real objective: the commercial center of Baltimore, which had far greater strategic importance than the largely symbolic capital city. But here, the British were turned back by resolute American resistance. In September they tried to attack Baltimore again, this time from the sea. Once more the attack foundered in the face of determined defense, in this case from Fort McHenry, which guards the entrance to Baltimore Harbor.

Three months later, Federalists from the New England states, where popular opinion had been strongly opposed to the conflict from the beginning, gathered secretly in Connecticut to share their reservations about "Mr. Madison's War." The Hartford Convention would consider—but eventually reject—motions that the New England states secede from the Union and make a separate peace with England. The delegates did agree, with an eye toward killing off the "Virginia Dynasty," to propose a Constitutional amendment prohibiting the election of a President from the same state twice in succession. This amendment was never ratified, and when news of the secret proceedings in Hartford later became public, the delegates were denounced as traitors, and the Federalist Party was effectively finished as a force in American politics.

MEANWHILE, FAR FROM THE GREAT LAKES AND BALTImore, a new front had opened in the South. In the summer of 1813, an ambitious Tennessee militia commander who felt the United States was entitled to the Spanish possessions south of Georgia had written to the War Department that he would "rejoice at the opportunity of placing the American eagle on the ramparts of Mobile, Pensacola, and Fort St. Augustine." Andrew Jackson was discouraged by Madison's reply—the equivalent of "Thanks, but no thanks"—but

Andrew Jackson, far right, commands the Battle of New Orleans from horseback

"Scarce a ball passed over, or fell short of its mark, but all striking full into his prospects for making war on the Indians brightened considerably when the Creek tribe rose up and massacred more than 500 settlers near Fort Mims, in what would later become Alabama. In a campaign that culminated in the Battle of Horseshoe Bend, Jackson and his militia hunted down and exterminated the Creek warriors so ruthlessly that the Tennessean was made a general in the U.S. Army and was instructed to defend New Orleans, a new target for the British that would give them control of the Mississippi.

Amid this flurry of events, peace negotiations at Ghent, Belgium, had been in progress for months. Finally, in December 1814, both sides decided they'd had enough. America renounced its interest in Canadian territory. The British, no longer strapped for manpower by the war against Napoleon, halted the practice of naval impressment. In the Treaty of Ghent, signed on Christmas Eve, 1814, both sides agreed to return to the status quo before the war's first shot was fired.

But the war's last shot had yet to be fired. The conflict had begun owing to a tardy communication; now it continued for the same reason. In the last week of December, British General Edward Pakenham prepared to assault New Orleans. But Andrew Jackson, fresh from slaughtering rebellious Native Americans, was waiting for him. Although Pakenham commanded 8,000 troops, a force more than double the size of Jackson's, the American general took brilliant advantage of the terrain, fortifying the earthen levees surrounding the city. The British charged these positions head on and were cut down mercilessly. In the space of a few hours, more than 2,000 British soldiers were killed, wounded or captured. Jackson suffered fewer than 100 casualties.

With this triumph, a conflict that had cost the United States much and gained it nothing concluded with a flourish. Yet the War of 1812 cannot be dismissed as an affair of sound and fury that signified nothing. Although it ended on a somber note for the British, they had secured Canada's future. And they had won a more important war, against Napoleon.

In America the war helped a new generation of leaders stake their claim to the future. Two heroes from the War of 1812—Andrew Jackson and William Henry Harrison—would later be elected President. Within five years, the Spanish colony of Florida would be annexed by the United States. And the Native American tribes east of the Mississippi would never again band together to present a united front against American expansion. Canada remained beyond America's reach, but the vast expanses of the West, stretching to the Pacific Ocean, were now open. ∎

the midst of our ranks " —George Gleig, British soldier, Battle of New Orleans

What So Proudly We Hailed

America's national anthem, *The Star-Spangled Banner,* salutes Old Glory from an unusual vantage point: the deck of a British warship

"THEN, IN THAT HOUR OF DELIVERANCE," Francis Scott Key would later recall, "my heart spoke. Does not such a country, and such defenders of their country, deserve a song?" The hour was the rain-swept gloom before dawn on the morning of Sept. 14, 1814. The deliverance was the successful American defense of Baltimore's vital port in the face of a British attack during one of the final battles of the War of 1812. And the song began with the words "O say can you see, by the dawn's early light ..."

Key was a prosperous Maryland lawyer and amateur poet who would watch the engagement from an unusual perch: the deck of a British warship flying a flag of truce. He and a friend, John S. Skinner, had sailed out to the British fleet under a white flag, in hopes of winning the release of Dr. William Beanes, a friend who had been taken prisoner earlier. Now the two men were held in custody, for the naval assault had begun.

An attack on the city by land had already failed. The new plan called for an assault from the water. The focal point for the British fleet would be Fort McHenry, which stood guard over the entrance to the harbor. Since the war's beginning, Major George Armistead, the commander of the fortress, had been preparing for just such a maneuver. But as he laid up stores of ammunition, Armistead also decided that he wanted a flag that would be visible from miles away, to friends and enemies alike. So, in the summer of 1813, Armistead hired Mary Young Pickersgill, a Baltimore widow who was a maker of nautical flags, to sew a version of the Stars and Stripes 30 ft. high and 42 ft. wide. She and her 13-year-old daughter worked for more than a month assembling the giant flag and were paid $405.90.

The British began bombarding Fort McHenry on the morning of Sept. 13 with long-range guns, mortars and rockets that exploded in spectacular bursts of shrapnel and fire. The colonials in the fort had no guns to match this ordnance, so they simply hunkered down to endure the pounding. After more than 18 hours of continual fire, the British ships finally approached the fort, ready to disgorge men through its breached walls and overrun the stronghold that was Baltimore's only defense. But Royal Navy commanders were astonished to find that when they came within range of Fort McHenry's guns, a thunderous fusillade erupted, disabling several of their ships and driving the rest backward.

Through the day and into the evening, Key and Skinner watched anxiously from aboard the truce ship on which they were detained, lying at anchor eight miles south of Fort McHenry. As darkness fell, intermittent flashes of shellfire briefly illuminated the small battle flag that Armistead had ordered flown over the fortress. Finally a rain squall enveloped the harbor, and the men lost sight of Fort McHenry's ramparts; they could only listen to the endless reports of the guns.

Early the next morning, Armistead watched the British fleet sail away; the Americans had won. Jubilant, he ordered his troops to hoist over the fort the large flag sewn by Mary Pickersgill a year earlier. Aboard the truce ship, Key and Skinner peered across the water as the rising sun burned off the predawn mist, and their hearts rose: a flag was still there.

Allowed to sail back to Baltimore as the British departed, Key took a letter from his pocket and began hastily jotting down the lines to a song he titled *The Defense of Fort McHenry*, choosing as his tune a British drinking song, *Anacreon in Heaven*. Within a few weeks, Key's lyrics had been published in newspapers around the nation, under a new title of uncertain origin: *The Star-Spangled Banner*. The poem-cum-song proved so popular that it quickly became America's unofficial national anthem, although its formal status as such was not formally ratified until 1931 ∎

The mammoth Fort McHenry flag at left is now being restored by the Smithsonian Institution. Below, the British fleet fires on the fortress in an early 19th century illustration. At right is Key's original manuscript version of his poem

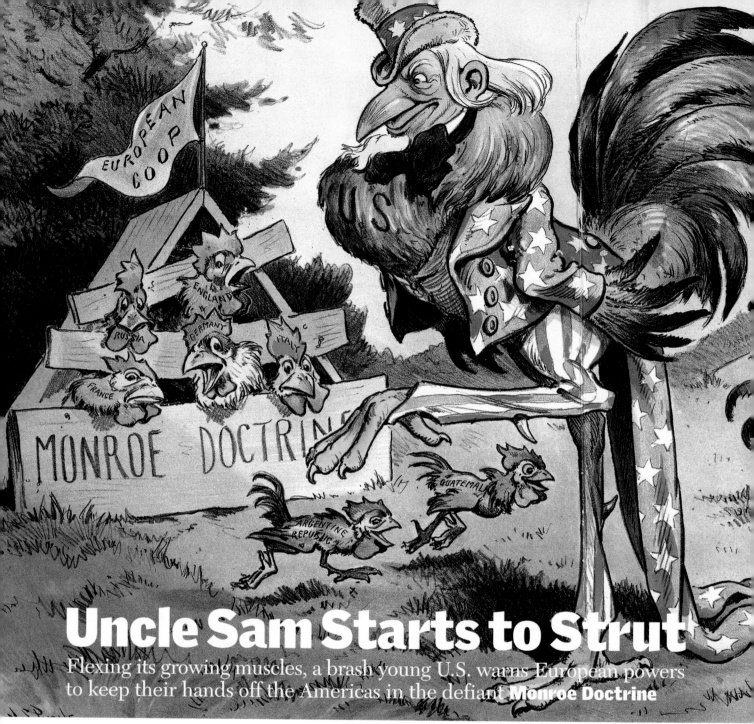

Uncle Sam Starts to Strut

Flexing its growing muscles, a brash young U.S. warns European powers to keep their hands off the Americas in the defiant **Monroe Doctrine**

THE EARLIEST RECORDED OCCURRENCE OF THE AMERICAN phenomenon we now call NIMBY—"not in my back yard"—came in December 1823, when James Monroe declared to Congress that "the American continents, by the free and independent condition which they have assumed and maintain, are henceforth not to be considered as subjects for future colonization by any European powers."

Thus began the Monroe Doctrine, the brainchild of John Quincy Adams, Monroe's Secretary of State. The hands-off manifesto bears the stamp of the adolescent young nation that put it forth: it's a muscular, in-your-face statement, a second declaration of independence that—in professing to speak

for all the nations of the Americas without bothering to solicit their input—made clear who was the cock o' the walk in the western hemisphere.

Like many historical doctrines (such as containment, the U.S. response to communist expansion after World War II), the Monroe Doctrine was a hastily improvised strategy for dealing with rapidly changing circumstances. In 1815, at the end of the War of 1812, there were only two fully independent nations anywhere in the western hemisphere: the U.S. and Haiti. Only seven years later, in 1822, a dozen independent new republics had sprouted in Central and South America, thanks to the revolutionary movements led by Simón Bolívar

"Our country may be likened to a new house. We lack many things, but we

Eight decades after the Monroe Doctrine was issued, the British humor magazine *Puck* lampooned U.S. swagger in a 1901 illustration

fered to form an alliance with Washington to keep rival powers (particularly France and Spain) out of the western hemisphere. But Adams argued persuasively that it would be "more dignified to avow our principles explicitly to Russia and France than to come in as a cockboat in the wake of the British man-of-war."

Monroe agreed and used his Annual Message to Congress to unveil a new policy that contained two warnings while also offering two assurances: no new colonies would be permitted in North or South America, although existing European colonies would be left undisturbed. And while any European interference in the western hemisphere would risk war with the U.S., Washington also promised not take sides in any European war. (Often forgotten today, this last point was important because U.S. public opinion was fixated at the time on Greece's struggle for independence from Turkey, and many Americans supported going to war to aid the Greeks.)

This combined ultimatum-promise managed to keep France, Spain and Russia out of the New World, although its success owed as much to the quiet backing of the Royal Navy as it did to American bluster. The flip side of the doctrine, which neither Adams nor Monroe ever envisioned, found the U.S. engaging in swaggering domination of Latin American nations. This strain of U.S. hegemony in the hemisphere would not emerge until the construction of a steel navy at the end of the 19th century, and the advent of Teddy Roosevelt's "gunboat diplomacy" at the dawn of the 20th. ∎

James Monroe

The headline on the July 12, 1817, edition of the Boston *Centinel*, which covered the triumphal tour of the country by new President James Monroe, proclaimed the dawn of a new "Era of Good Feelings." The phrase could have summed up Monroe's life as neatly as it did his term in office. Born to a prosperous family of Virginia farmers in 1758, Monroe left the College of William and Mary in 1776, while still a teenager, to join the Continental Army. Commissioned a junior officer, he was seriously wounded at the Battle of Trenton but rose to the rank of major before the war's end. Afterward, he served as a Virginia delegate to the Constitutional Convention, where he was one of the faction that held out for the inclusion of the Bill of Rights in the document.

The last of the "Virginia Dynasty" that included four of the first five U.S. Presidents, Monroe was beloved by his countrymen. Thomas Jefferson, his mentor, once said that his fellow Virginian was "so honest that if you turned his soul inside out there would not be a spot on it." Monroe was elected President by a large majority in 1816 and was returned to office in 1820 almost unanimously. Buoyed by a booming economy and still lit by the glow of the triumph of the War of 1812, the eight years Monroe spent in office were an expansive, dynamic era in America. He oversaw the Missouri Compromise that brought Missouri and Maine into the Union, as well as the annexation of Spain's holdings in Florida. The Federalist Party dwindled to insignificance during his first term, allowing Monroe to preside over a one-party nation devoid of ideological rancor. Sharing the exquisitely timed exit strategy of Jefferson and Adams, Monroe died on July 4, 1831, the 55th anniversary of the Declaration of Independence. His death marked the passing of America's original Greatest Generation: he was the last President who had fought in the Revolution.

and his fellow "liberators" under the inspiration of the U.S., and the only European colonies remaining in the New World were Canada, Belize, Bolivia and the Guineas.

The European powers were determined to take back at least some of their recently lost territory, while other nations (especially Russia) were ambitious to carve new colonies out of the American West. Strangely enough, the British, masters of the world's largest empire, were delighted by the rising tide of anticolonialism on the far side of the Atlantic. Their hold on Canada was secure, and their vast merchant fleets were finding important new markets in the southern Americas, where trade had formerly been restricted by Spain. Britain even of-

possess the most precious of all—liberty!" —James Monroe

Struggling to Stay United

As the years pass, the divisions between slave and free states threaten to split the Union in two, but the **Missouri Compromise** patches things up

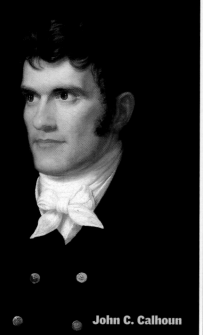

John C. Calhoun

Henry Clay

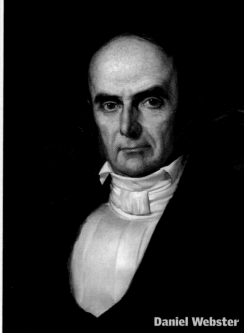

Daniel Webster

LIKE TWO DANCE PARTNERS WHO DESPISE EACH OTHER but must put on a show of harmony for an expectant audience, America's Northern and Southern states found themselves locked in an awkward embrace 4 decades into their marriage. The "mystic chords of memory" that Abraham Lincoln would later refer to still sounded in the background, appealing to their sense of a shared past and the need to maintain the glorious Union they had won in the Revolution. But the issue of slavery increasingly pulled them apart. And in 1820, when the Missouri Territory tapped these partners on the shoulder, requesting admission into the Union as a slave state, it seemed that the music was finally about to stop.

For almost 30 years, the expansion of the Union had proceeded at a deliberate pace, guided by an unspoken but effective understanding: for each new free state that was admitted to the Union, a slaveholding state would follow. Neither faction would be permitted to add more than one additional state until the other had matched it. So it was that after the original 13 states had ratified the Constitution, Vermont alternated with Kentucky, Tennessee with Ohio, Louisiana with Indiana, and Mississippi with Illinois.

The admission of Alabama, in 1819, brought the Union into almost perfect balance: the 22 states were divided evenly between free and slaveholding governments. The former camp had a total population of slightly more than 5 million (with 105 seats in the House of Representatives), while the latter encompassed almost 4.5 million people (and controlled 81 seats in the House).

After Alabama was admitted, it was the turn of the free states to expand their membership. So the Northern camp was outraged when the slaveholding states moved to admit Missouri before the free states had added to their number. Acceding to this request would hand the slave states an outright majority in the Senate and bolster their numbers in the House of Representatives—as well as set a dangerous precedent for congressional approval of slavery's expansion to territory far outside its traditional Southern base. In short, the move to admit Missouri was perceived by the Northern bloc as a treacherous act of aggression, destabilizing a system that had been carefully calculated to sustain the Union.

So the free states answered with aggression of their own: Representative James Tallmadge of New York sponsored a bill that would ban further importation of slaves into Missouri and require that all children of slave parents be freed by age 25, acts that would transform Missouri into a free state within decades. The House, dominated by non–slave states, quickly passed the measure. In the Senate, Rufus King, also of New York, argued that Congress was empowered to ban slavery in any new state. William Pinkey of Maryland replied that new states had the same rights of self-determination as the original 13. The Senate, tied between free and slave states, deadlocked on both pieces of legislation.

"This momentous question, like a fire bell in the night, awakened and filled

The bitter debate went on for three months, and Northern states began to rumble ominously about seceding from the Union. Finally, a truce was brokered by Henry Clay, the Speaker of the House, already known as "the Great Compromiser." Missouri would enter the Union as a slave state, but its admission would be delayed until the territory of Maine (which had recently broken away from Massachusetts) had first entered as a free state. Additionally, no new states formed from land acquired in the Louisiana Purchase would, under any circumstances, become slave states if any part of their territory was situated above the 36° 30´ line of latitude. (The one exception to this rule would be Missouri itself, whose southern border is the 36° 30´ line.) New states below this boundary would be permitted to decide the issue of slavery for themselves. Abolitionists were comforted by the fact that the Southern power grab had been stopped. Proponents of states' rights savored the victory for self-determination. And representatives of states dependent on slave labor felt clever about having bargained away the territory of the Great Plains north of Missouri, which was ill-suited to plantation farming.

While the Speaker worked to deliver the House of Representatives, Daniel Webster, an abolitionist Senator from Massachusetts, came to the conclusion that compromise was preferable to seeing the Union split apart and reluctantly endorsed Clay's compromise—bringing with him enough Senators to ensure passage in the upper house. Within the Monroe Administration, Secretary of War John C. Calhoun

(formerly a Congressman from South Carolina) was relieved that the cause of the slave states had not been seriously damaged, and he begin lobbying for presidential approval.

I N MARCH 1820, BOTH SIDES RELUCTANTLY SIGNED OFF ON Clay's bargain. Like any good compromise, this one made all parties concerned miserable. Southerners hated the precedent that had been set: Congress had now established that it could make laws regulating and limiting the spread of slavery. And Northerners remained angry and bitter about any expansion of slavery outside the confines of the deep South. But even with the widespread unhappiness it engendered, Clay's Missouri Compromise would hold the Union together for an additional three decades.

During these years, the elaborate two-step between North and South resumed: Arkansas entered the Union as a slave state, followed by Michigan as a free state. Then Florida and Iowa, Texas and Wisconsin, and so on. When the music stopped once more, in 1850, Clay, by then 70 years old, would again collaborate with Webster and Calhoun to broker a compromise that averted civil war, but only for a decade.

Yet even in 1820, everyone knew that something had changed. The problem was too intractable, the situation had veered too close to disaster, and the resolution seemed only to postpone an inevitable catastrophe. "I take it for granted that the present question is a mere preamble," wrote John Quincy Adams that year, "a title page to a great, tragic volume." ■

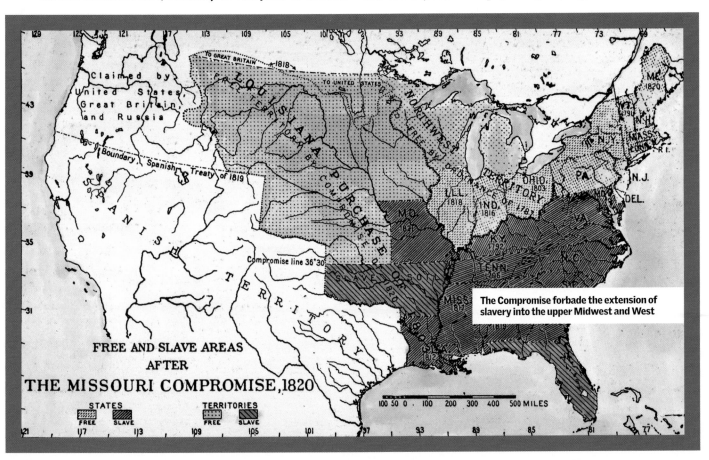

FREE AND SLAVE AREAS
AFTER
THE MISSOURI COMPROMISE, 1820

STATES   TERRITORIES
FREE   SLAVE   FREE   SLAVE

100 50 0 . 100   200   300   400   500 MILES

The Compromise forbade the extension of slavery into the upper Midwest and West

"one with terror ... the death knell of the Union." —Thomas Jefferson, 1820

Erie Canal

"I've got a mule, her name is Sal/ Fifteen miles on the Erie Canal./ Low bridge, everybody down!/ Low bridge, for we're goin' through a town." —Folk song

Clinton's Big Ditch

Busting through mountains, straddling streams and dazzling onlookers with its complicated system of locks that bent New York State's hilly hinterlands to its will, the Erie Canal was a paradigm-shattering wonder of transportation when it opened in the mid-1820s.

You might also say it was a really big ditch. In fact, doubters called the proposed canal "Clinton's Big Ditch" after its chief booster, New York Governor DeWitt Clinton, a former mayor of New York City. For variety's sake, they also labeled it "Clinton's Folly." Nor were they alone: long years before, when the notion of just such a canal had crossed Thomas Jefferson's desk, he labeled it "little short of madness." Yet Clinton saw his vision of a waterway connecting New York City to the Great Lakes completed, after eight years of construction, on Nov. 4, 1825, when, after an inaugural cruise (above), he poured a keg of water from Lake Erie into the waters off Manhattan.

A classic example of the power of thinking big, the 363-mile-long waterway reflects the urgent energies that were powering the young nation into a period of continental expansion. Here was a dream large enough to match the vast reaches of the former Northwest Territory it now made easily accessible. Where once teams of oxen and mules had strained to haul wagons loaded with goods uphill and down in the rolling Allegheny Mountains, far larger quantities of merchandise now floated serenely through the landscape, mule-drawn on towpaths. The canal was an immediate success, dropping the cost of transporting a ton of goods from Buffalo to New York City from $100 to $10. Within a year of the canal's opening, an estimated 2,000 boats, 9,000 horses and mules and 8,000 men were employed along its route.

The canal was an engineering marvel; it marshalled 83 locks to counter its vertical rise of 675 ft., while 18 aqueducts carried barges similar to the modern tourist boat pictured here over rivers and streams, and numerous bridges took them directly through upstate New York cities. And the commerce it fostered, as Clinton had predicted, made New York City by far the nation's most prosperous port. Big ditch? More like Big Rich. ∎

Looming Changes for Women

Shedding the rigid confines of a society that offers few opportunities, the **"Lowell Girls"** of New England's textile factories strive for freedom

IF THE PAGES OF THIS BOOK APPEAR TO COMPOSE A PARADE of men's faces—well, welcome to the 18th century. The new nation being created in America was dedicated to the proposition that all men are created equal—and all women are not. For even in this new "egalitarian" society some things had not changed: women and non-property holders were second-class citizens; blacks and Native Americans, third. Yet the age promised to end old constraints. Breathing the air of independence, Abigail Adams wrote to her husband, "If particular care and attention is not paid to the ladies, we are determined to foment a rebellion, and will not hold ourselves bound by any laws in which we have no vote or representation."

At this time, a woman's horizons were tightly constricted:

she grew up in her father's house, received some education—if her father could afford it, and definitely not too much—then entered into marriage, becoming her husband's "helpmate" and the mother of his children. Outside this rigid path, for those who did not marry, only a few opportunities presented themselves: to work as a teacher, a governess, a companion or a caregiver. So rigid were society's gender divisions that amid all the debates, all the resolutions, all the *Federalist* papers that examined the nature of democratic government, one finds no sentence in which it is proposed that women ought to have the right to be represented. In fact, women did not receive the vote in America until 1920, following decades of protests, petitions and lobbying.

"Come and ... have the credit as well as the advantage of perfecting the first

Supervised by men, women work in a textile factory in 1834. Inset: Samuel Slater, who created the first American water-powered mill

Slater sailed to America in 1789, having memorized the workings of Arkwright's machines, and when he heard that Moses Brown, a Quaker merchant, trader and industrialist in Rhode Island, was trying to develop textile mills based on British models, he wrote to Brown, received an encouraging reply and soon joined him. Slater convinced Brown to build new machines to his designs, and their enterprise flourished. Even as Slater was helping create the first water-powered American textile mill, his wife Hannah achieved a breakthrough of a different kind: in 1793 she became the first woman to file for a patent in the new U.S. patent office. She had invented a new way to spin thread.

The achievements of Slater and Brown in Pawtucket, R.I., were soon matched by a member of a prominent Massachusetts family, Francis Lowell. Touring British cotton mills on a trip abroad in 1810, Lowell remembered enough of the workings of the big spinning machines to found his own plant on his return; with his partner, master mechanic Paul Moody, he built in Waltham, Mass., the first American mill that carded, spun thread and wove cloth under one roof.

BUSINESS IN THE LOWELL PLANTS BOOMED THROUGH THE 1820s and accelerated even more rapidly in the following decades. As the factories grew, so did their demand for labor, and it was to these textile mills that young farm women from around New England went, searching for something that few American women had ever known before: a job, a paycheck, an existence independent of the strictures of a father or a husband. To read today about the disciplines they willingly accepted—a 12-hour workday, six days a week; communal living in closely chaperoned dormitories—is to realize how desperately these women needed to escape from the roles that restricted them, or the poverty that starved them.

The owners of these factories, well aware that no father at this time would send his daughter off to live unsupervised, ensured the strictest oversight of their workers, the "Lowell Girls." The mills owned not only the factories but also the dormitories, shops, banks and churches of the town. Under the "Lowell Plan," the women who had been released from their long workday ate family-style meals together, observed a strict dress code and were able to attend evening lectures on religious and educational topics. Eventually they operated their own journal, the Lowell *Offering*.

Soon, women were participating in another aspect of labor. Where there are owners and laborers, there will be strikes and strife. As early as 1824, some of the female textile workers at the plants in Pawtucket joined their male counterparts in one of America's earliest large labor strikes, initiated to halt wage cuts. The "Lowell Girls" would go on strike in 1834, 1836 and again in 1846. The women's rebellion that Abigail Adams promised John Adams had come to pass, but this revolution marched to the sound of a spinning loom rather than a fife and drum. ∎

The first notice that women might play a new role in society arrived as the product not of politics but of industry. In fact, this breakthrough can be traced to the dawn of the Industrial Revolution in America, with the development of cotton mills in New England that began hiring young women to operate their machines. This revolution was the product of two ambitious men: Samuel Slater, a British immigrant to America, and a successful U.S. businessman, Frances Cabot Lowell

Slater was a young man from Derbyshire who learned the details of the revolutionary spinning machine, invented by Richard Arkwright while an apprentice in a British mill.

watermill in America." —Moses Brown to Samuel Slater, 1790

Sunnyside

"My heart yearns for home; I begrudge every [year] that I am obliged to pass

separated from my cottage and my kindred." —Irving, letter, 1845

An American Artist

Imagining the generations that would follow the Revolution, John Adams once wrote, "I must study politics and war that my sons may have liberty to study mathematics and philosophy. My sons ought to study mathematics and philosophy, geography, natural history and naval architecture ... in order to give their children a right to study painting, poetry, music, architecture, statuary, tapestry and porcelain." Adams might have been looking forward to a writer like Washington Irving, whose first name alone declares him a member of the generation that followed the Founding Fathers. Irving was the first American to earn his living as a man of letters; his success allowed him to purchase the lovely home pictured here, Sunnyside, which basks on the Hudson River in the area Irving made famous in two classic tales, *Rip Van Winkle* and *The Legend of Sleepy Hollow*.

Irving was not only America's first great writer; he was also the first to adapt America's heritage and lore as his subject matter, finding fertile ground for his pen in the bygone days when New York, under Dutch rule, was New Amsterdam. In his first works, including *A History of New York* (1809), Irving wrote in the crisp, satirical style of such British wits as Addison and Steele, signing his work with the pseudonym Dietrich Knickerbocker. By the time he published *The Sketch Book of Geoffrey Crayon, Gent.* in 1820, he had turned toward the Romantic style popular in Europe, which celebrated old folk tales, supernatural themes and picturesque locales.

The author's life straddled a great swath of American history; he was born in 1783, the year the U.S. won its independence in the Treaty of Paris; he died in 1859, with the nation on the eve of civil war. His work also painted a broad picture of the nation; turning to nonfiction, he traveled to the West, chronicling his adventures in *A Tour on the Prairies* (1835), then wrote a highly successful five-volume biography of his eponym, George Washington (1855-59). As John Adams would have appreciated, Irving was a cartographer of sorts: he was the first to put America on the world's literary map. ■

Jackson, inset left, and Adams, right, waged a bitter campaign. This cartoon lampoons "Old Hickory's" tough military discipline; its caption reads, "Jackson is to be President and you will be hanged." The pro-Jackson handbill at right, from the 1828 election, recounts the saga of 1824 in rhyme

The Purloined Electors

In the divisive **Election of 1824,** Andrew Jackson wins the popular vote, but John Quincy Adams is handed the presidency in a "corrupt bargain"

IMAGINE A BITTERLY CONTESTED NATIONAL ELECTION—IN which the rhetoric is as much about personalities as issues—that yields an inconclusive result at the polls, leading to a politically brokered resolution and widespread charges that the presidency was "stolen." If this scenario seems familiar, then it is further proof of Harry Truman's adage that "the only thing new in the world is the history you don't

know." For the election described here took place in 1824.

That year is carved into the headstone atop the grave of the "Era of Good Feelings" over which James Monroe presided. The near unanimous re-election of the last member of the "Virginia Dynasty" in 1820 masked the deep divisions that were percolating just beneath the surface of American society. Even though there was but one political party, the Democratic-

"I cannot believe that killing 2,500 Englishmen at New Orleans qualifies

Republicans, that fielded candidates for the election of 1824, the four candidates who vied for its backing embodied the tensions that were about to engulf the nation.

John Quincy Adams, Secretary of State to the outgoing President, was the son of former President John Adams and a New England, upper-class conservative. William H. Crawford, Monroe's Treasury Secretary, was a well-heeled Georgia lawyer who aspired to the mantle of Southern leadership once held by Washington, Jefferson, Madison and Monroe. Andrew Jackson, favorite son of Tennessee, was a popular hero of the War of 1812 who claimed to speak for the emerging states of the West. His rival for this title, Henry Clay of Kentucky, was the Speaker of the House of Representatives.

The rivalries to which these candidates gave voice were in large measure regional: Northern and Southern voters squared off against one another, with slave-holding states still feeling vulnerable in the wake of 1820's Missouri Compromise (which limited the growth of slavery), and Northern-state industrialists weary of trying to compete against businesses that paid no wages. But a geographical division was also emerging. The Americans in the Western frontier states—not only Tennessee and Kentucky but also Missouri, Indiana, Illinois and Ohio—felt they were considered inferior by the more established, original states along the Eastern Seaboard.

New voters were also coming to the polls: by 1824, all but a few states had repealed laws that restricted voting to property owners (although laws that limited voting to white males remained firmly in place). Additionally, most states had dropped indirect selection of members of the Electoral College, allowing the public to vote directly for presidential electors. As a result, more than 100,000 new voters would come to the polls in 1824 (an increase of more than 130% over the total vote count in 1820), and many of them were Americans of modest means who felt that the "common man" needed representation.

Modern politicians, so often accused of gratuitous partisanship, would gag at the level of slander that quickly came to dominate the 1824 campaign. Jackson was accused of being a murderer and his wife an adulteress, while Adams was branded a closet monarchist and Clay was labeled an alcoholic and compulsive gambler. Only Crawford, who had suffered a massive stroke early in the campaign and was thus deemed no longer to be a threat to any of the others, was spared.

Adams and Jackson quickly overshadowed the prickly

PRESIDENCY!!!

This is the House that We built.

TREASURY.

This is the malt that lay in the House that WE Built.

John Q. Adams,

This is the *MAIDEN* all forlorn, who worried herself from night till morn, to enter the House that We built.

CLAY,

This is the *MAN* all tattered and torn, who courted the maiden all forlorn, who worried herself from night till morn to enter the House that We built.

WEBSTER,

This is the *PRIEST*, all shaven and shorn, that married the man all tattered and torn, unto the maiden all forlorn, who worried herself from night till morn, to enter the House that We Built.

CONGRESS,

This is the BEAST, that carried the Priest all shaven and shorn, who married the man all tattered and torn, unto the maiden all forlorn, who worried herself from night till morn, to enter the House that We Built.

CABINET,

These are the *Rats* that pulled off their hats, and joined the Beast that carried the Priest all shaven and shorn, who married the man all tattered and torn unto the maiden all forlorn who worried herself from night till morn to enter the House that We built.

"OLD HICKORY,"

This is the *Wood*, well season'd and good, We will use as a rod to whip out the RATS, that pulled off their hats and joined the Beast that carried the Priest all shaven and shorn, who married the man all tattered and torn, unto the maiden all forlorn, who worried herself from night till morn, to enter the House that We Built.

NEW-YORK.

This is the *state*, both early and late, that will strengthen the Wood well seasoned and good, to be used as a rod to whip out Rats that pulled off their hats, and joined the beast that carried the Priest, all shaven and shorn, who married the man all tattered and torn unto the maiden all forlorn, who worried herself from night till morn to enter the House that We Built.

EBONY & TOPAZ.

*The People.

Clay, but neither was able to attract the constitutionally required majority of votes on Election Day: Jackson garnered slightly more than 43% of the popular vote and 99 electoral votes, while Adams took a bit more than 31% of the popular vote and 84 electoral votes. Under the Constitution, this meant that the election would be decided in the House of Representatives. And that meant that the previously eclipsed Henry Clay (who presided over the House as Speaker) was back in the driver's seat.

Because Clay had polled a distant fourth (behind even the disabled Crawford), he didn't dare to attempt making himself President. But he did resolve to wring maximum advantage from his position. At first glance, his fellow Westerner, Andrew Jackson, seemed like the obvious choice. But Clay knew that among Western political leaders, any advance for Jackson's ambitions would be an impediment to his own. Moreover, Clay had sincere reservations about Jackson, whom he suspected of being too hot-headed to lead the Republic.

Just as Alexander Hamilton had intervened in the House's decision in 1800, swinging votes away from his personal rival Aaron Burr to Thomas Jefferson, Clay now delivered his votes to Adams—enough of them to hand him the presidency on the first ballot in the House, on Feb. 9, 1825, if only by a margin of one state. Days later, Adams named his new Secretary of State: Henry Clay. Jackson supporters quickly labeled the appointment the culmination of a "corrupt bargain" secretly struck between Adams and Clay. Jackson wrote at the time, "So you see, the Judas of the West has closed the contract and will receive the 30 pieces of silver."

Adams took office but presided unhappily for only a single term, much of which was taken up with lingering partisan bitterness and attacks that presaged the next election. Jackson ran for the presidency again in 1828 and won by a large margin. And the Democratic-Republican Party, like the Federalist Party before it, simply imploded. Jackson assumed leadership of a new party, the Democrats, who aspired to speak for the common man. Adams and his conservative allies formed the Whig Party, which would endure for only a few decades before being superseded by the group we now know as Republicans. But the most enduring legacy of the election of 1824 is that it marked the beginning of a power shift—from the established interests of the older states on the Atlantic seaboard to the new, emerging states of the West—that continues to this day. ■

[Jackson] for the ... duties of the First Magistracy." —Henry Clay, 1824

Discipline and Disguise

To walk through the door of Monticello is to step inside Thomas Jefferson's mind: seldom has a home better reflected the temperament of its owner. Then again, how many homes are designed by their owner—and then obsessively perfected by him over a period of five decades? Jefferson inherited the Virginia mountaintop property on which he would build this classically inspired villa when he was 21. Six years later he began its construction, and when he died 54 years later, he was still tinkering with its elegant capstone.

Jefferson not only designed Monticello; he built it with wood sawed from his trees, bricks formed from his earth and stones dug from the soil of his "little mountain" (*monticello,* in Italian). He stocked it with all the tools of Enlightenment living: books from around the world, wines from France, specimens from the American West and home improvements of his own design, like his reading chair with candleholders built into the arms.

Pleasing as the prospect of Monticello is, what we can't see is just as interesting. Many great Southern homes of this era were surrounded by outbuildings: slave quarters, stables and storehouses. And so is this building—except that Jefferson carefully planned a pair of long outbuildings , or "dependencies," built into the sides of the hill where it falls away behind the mansion. Underground passageways connect the two large outbuildings to the main residence, obscuring from view the entire support apparatus on which the great home depended. That's yet another reason why Monticello is such an apt reflection of the deeply complex man biographer Joseph Ellis called an "American Sphinx." In 1998, DNA tests on members of a black family who had long claimed descent from Jefferson through a relationship with his one-quarter-black slave, Sally Hemings, lent scientific credence to their contention. When such rumors surfaced in Jefferson's time, he vehemently denied them. As in his tucked-away outbuildings at Monticello, the man who wrote the Declaration of Independence may have preferred to leave some dependencies undeclared. ∎

Monticello

"where I hope my days will end, at Monticello." —Thomas Jefferson

Inside Monticello

Bedroom

Passageway

Book Room

Hidden Connections

Above is one of the two underground passageways that connect the outbuildings to the main home. At the ends of the hidden "dependencies" two small cottages flank the residence: a law office and a "honeymoon cottage" where Jefferson and his wife Martha lived while the home was under construction. Martha died of complications of childbirth in 1782, when she was only 33, leaving Jefferson a widower for most of his adult life—a tragedy that ensured the home reflected only its owner's taste.

A dedicated student of natural history, Jefferson kept all sorts of specimens at Monticello, with pride of place going to the Native American artifacts sent back by Meriwether Lewis and William Clark on their Western travels, right. Skins and antlers decked the halls, while fossilized mammoth bones greeted visitors in the entrance hall.

A Life of the Mind

In one of his more creative gestures, Jefferson placed his bed in an alcove between his bedroom and his small study, which is visible on the far side of the bed in the picture above. Although his bedroom was drenched by sunshine pouring through one of the home's 11 skylights (an innovation to America that he borrowed from the French), Jefferson boasted in his old age that the sun had not caught him in bed for 50 years.

The view at right is from Monticello's "book room" to the bedroom study, where Jefferson kept a bust of his friend (and sometime political adversary), John Adams. Books were everywhere in the home; Jefferson sold some 10,000 volumes to the nation after the British burned Washington, D.C., in 1814, and they became the foundation of the Library of Congress.

Gallery

Kitchen

Upstairs, Downstairs

In Monticello's kitchen, right, slaves created dishes inspired by Jefferson's long residence in France; he arranged for one of his chefs to be tutored in the art of French cuisine in Annapolis, Md. Visiting the home in 1824, Daniel Webster remarked that the dishes were "served in half Virginian, half French style, in good taste and abundance." In colonial and Revolutionary times, only two meals were taken a day: an early breakfast and a large dinner in the late afternoon.

Eight recipes used at Monticello survive in Jefferson's handwriting. The table was supplied by herbs and vegetables grown in Jefferson's garden; a student of horticulture, he collected, imported and cultivated many varieties of plants. Perhaps the nation's foremost oenophile in his day, he grew many varieties of wine grapes in his vineyards and designed a system to deliver wine from his belowground cellars to the dining room, via dumbwaiters tucked inside the fireplace mantel.

How Monticello reflects Jefferson:
His obsessions, his contradictions, his brilliance

MIRROR OF THE MAN

He placed his mind, like his house, on a lofty height, whence he might contemplate the whole universe," an admiring French aristocrat wrote of Thomas Jefferson. Today, Monticello is a restored testament to Jefferson's exacting vision. But in 1768 that lofty height outside Charlottesville, Va., was a wildly impractical place for a compulsively practical man to start building a home. After a lifetime of "putting up and pulling down," as he called it, Jefferson completed his personal universe, but he died still enslaving dozens who had built it for him.

▲ **Top, Jefferson's sketch for the original Monticello**

Innovative

Jefferson was captivated by the view from his mountain and didn't want it cluttered with outbuildings. His elegant solution was to use the slope of the hilltop to conceal the structures—kitchen, smokehouse, stables, icehouse, brewery, laundry—in a pair of wings extending from each side of the main house. From above, these **dependencies** form wide, L-shaped terraces. From below, the rooms open to the hillside and connect to the house by a **covered passage** that continues under the main house

The roof has 11 skylights

The dome was a first for an American house

Dining room

Dependencies

Main house

Dependencies

A passionate **gardener**, Jefferson also meticulously planned every landscape detail

Garden walk

Fish pond

Vegetable garden

Mulberry row (slave quarters)

Newlyweds Thomas and Martha Jefferson lived in this small building while the main house was under construction

Time Graphic by Ed Gabel and Jackson Dykman

JEFFERSON STARTED BUILDING MONTICELLO WHEN HE WAS 25 ...

Adaptive

Jefferson's first design for Monticello was a reflection of the classical Italian **architecture** he had studied in books. When he began building the second, larger house, he incorporated contemporary ideas he had seen in France, such as skylights to illuminate interior spaces

Two features in particular—the **dome** and the tall **east windows**—are a nod to the Hôtel de Salm, a house Jefferson admired in Paris

Efficient

Jefferson designed even the smallest details of Monticello "with a greater eye to convenience"

The **weather vane** atop the east portico has an indicator that can be read from any of the front windows

The **clock** in the entrance hall also marks the days of the week along the wall

A **dumbwaiter** connects the dining room to the wine cellar directly below

Puzzling

The first floor has grand rooms but no grand staircase. Jefferson saw such things as a waste of space, so he tucked very **narrow, steep staircases** at each end of the central hall. Fine for him: he lived on the first floor. But women wearing long dresses or carrying a baby or a tray faced a dangerous climb

The **octagonal room** under the dome is perhaps the house's most striking space. But what was it for? Not much, apparently. It briefly served as a **bedroom** for Jefferson's grandson but most often was just **storage space**. One problem: those treacherous stairs make it hard to get large pieces of furniture up there

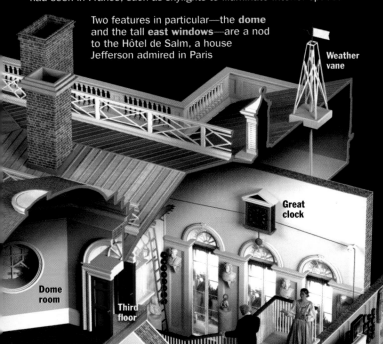

Weather vane

Great clock

Dome room

Third floor

Family sitting room

East front windows continue up to second floor, creating illusion from outside that house is only one story

Second floor

Stairs

Privy

Book room

Venetian porch

Parlor

Jefferson's bedroom

Greenhouse

Study

Venetian porch

Personal

Jefferson devoted nearly a third of the main level to his **private apartment.** He rarely admitted visitors to this area, as it was perfectly tailored to his pursuits: a study where he maintained voluminous correspondence (even using a machine called a polygraph to copy letters as he wrote them); a collection of scientific instruments for studying the weather and the stars; a greenhouse for cultivating new plants; and, most important, space for his vast library

Sources:
Thomas Jefferson Foundation (*monticello.org*); *The Worlds of Thomas Jefferson at Monticello,* by Susan R. Stein; *Monticello in Measured Drawings,* commentary by William L. Beiswanger; *Thomas Jefferson's Monticello; Jefferson and Monticello: The Biography of a Builder,* by

... HE ADDED THE FINAL TOUCHES WHEN HE WAS 80 YEARS OLD

A Time for Reflection

The lives of John Adams and Thomas Jefferson resemble the two coiled strands that make up the signature double helix of DNA: they are intertwined and interconnected, and the imprint of their collaboration shapes the future. In the tension of their ongoing political duels—Adams the pragmatic advocate of a strong central government, Jefferson the idealistic champion of the common man—we can trace the origin of one of the enduring debates of American history.

There is a wonderful shapeliness as well to the relationship of the two. They began as friends and colleagues, became strongly divided by deeply held political convictions, then weathered their anger and spite to become, in later years, once again the greatest of friends; their correspondence in their last years is one of history's great epistolary duets. The moments they shared together make up a mini-history of the founding decades of the U.S.: shaping the immortal words that declared America's independence in 1776; touring the gardens of France together as fellow U.S. diplomats in the 1780s; waging a bitter war of vitriol through their surrogates in the press during Adams' term as President—while Jefferson was his Vice President—in the 1790s. Even the moments they spent apart are telling: when Jefferson took office in 1801, Adams, his beaten rival, sneaked out of Washington at 4 in the morning of the Inauguration rather than see his foe triumphant. As for another absence: Adams, devoid of illusions, might not be surprised that Jefferson is honored in the fine memorial shown here, while there is no Adams Memorial in Washington.

After Jefferson's inauguration, the two antagonists remained silent for long years, but they began corresponding again in 1812, brought together by the efforts of an old mutual friend, Dr. Benjamin Rush. Over the next 14 years, they exchanged 158 letters. "You and I ought not to die," Adams wrote Jefferson, "before we have explained ourselves to each other." That they did, memorably; and then, in a final showering of grace upon the nation they had helped create, the two statesmen died, hours apart, on July 4, 1826, the 50th anniversary of the Declaration of Independence. ■

Jefferson Memorial

upon our ancient terms of goodwill." —John Adams, 1820